Airpower Leadership on the Front Line

Lt Gen George H. Brett and Combat Command

Douglas A. Cox
Lieutenant Colonel, USAF

Air University Press
Maxwell Air Force Base, Alabama

September 2006

Air University Library Cataloging Data

Cox, Douglas A., 1967-
    Airpower leadership on the front line : Lieutenant General George H. Brett and combat command / Douglas A. Cox.
      p. ; cm.
    Includes bibliographical references and index.
    ISBN: 978-1-78039-203-5
    1. Brett, George H. (George Howard), 1886–1963—Military leadership. 2. Command of troops. 3. Generals—United States—Biography. 4. United States. Army Air Forces—Biography. I. Title.

    358.40092—dc22

Disclaimer

Air University Press
131 West Shumacher Avenue
Maxwell AFB AL 36112-6615
http://aupress.maxwell.af.mil

Contents

Illustrations

CONTENTS

iv

Foreword

With *Airpower Leadership on the Front Line: Lt Gen George H. Brett and Combat Command*, Douglas Cox makes a singular contribution to American airpower biography. Books abound on personalities that reach high rank and whose careers culminate in great success. These studies often glean keen insight about leadership style, and some are vocationally valuable as examples of effective command. But the analysis of history's great winners yields something less than a full dimensional sense of leadership. The examination of those men and women who do not quite reach exalted status can flesh out the lessons of effective leadership.

This is what Cox does here. George H. Brett certainly reached high rank, and only the most cynical and uninformed observer would judge his career a failure. Yet World War II did not propel him along the same career trajectory of a Curtis LeMay or a Hoyt Vandenberg or a Jimmy Doolittle. Why? For all kinds of reasons; some of which were good, some bad, some within Brett's control, and others entirely outside his purview. Through a careful examination of primary and secondary sources, as well as his own acumen as a sharp officer, Cox uses Brett's life to illuminate those factors that at first sped Brett through the ranks and then those variables that appeared to block his further advancement. Cox reminds us of what we often know intuitively but often forget intellectually: that success has many fathers, including personal luck and fortuitous circumstance. *Airpower Leadership on the Front Line* pulls no punches regarding Brett's limitations, but it also acknowledges broader factors at play in his career. In the end, Cox delineates those factors that make for successful leaders; and, more importantly, suggests which among those variables are within a person's control and hence worthy of attention and energy. As much as studies of commanders who grabbed the brass ring, this examination of George H. Brett adds insight into the makings of effective leadership and successful command.

THOMAS HUGHES
Associate Professor
School of Advanced Air and
    Space Studies
Air University

About the Author

Lt Col Douglas A. Cox is a B-52 radar navigator and weapons officer. A 1989 graduate of the United States Air Force Academy (USAFA), he was one of the first USAFA cadets to major in English. He has been assigned to Wurtsmith AFB, Michigan; Castle AFB, California; and Minot AFB, North Dakota, as a B-52 crew-member. His last assignment before attending Air Command and Staff College, Maxwell AFB, Alabama, was as a member of the Air Warfare Center staff at Nellis AFB, Nevada. He has over 2,500 hours in the B-52G and H models. His interest in writing and literature led him to a fascination with airpower history, particularly the leadership challenges faced by the top Airmen in World War II. In June of 2004 he was assigned to a B-52 bomb squadron at Barksdale AFB, Louisiana, as a squadron operations officer. Colonel Cox is graced by the companionship of his lovely wife, Lynae, and his two sons, Allen and Steven.

Acknowledgments

This book was fun to write and even more fun to research. Without the generous help and support of a long list of experts and friends this would not have been the case. My thesis adviser, Dr. David Mets, inspired this project and brought his sage advice and insight to its execution. His energy and expertise transformed impossibilities into tasks completed. My thesis reader, Dr. Thomas Hughes, lent his unerring sense of style and his gifted historical perspective to the project and his amicable encouragement to me personally. Col Larry Thompson receives my thanks for connecting me with his friend, Lt Gen Devol "Rock" Brett, USAF, retired, without whose unstinting assistance this project would have been immensely more difficult; General Brett freely shared his valuable time, keen memory, airpower insight, and obtains my highest gratitude. Thanks are also due to another retired Air Force general officer, Maj Gen John Huston, professor emeritus, United States Naval Academy, who went to considerable personal inconvenience to provide me with rare documents saved by Lt Gen George H. Brett covering the relatively obscure American, Dutch, British, and Australian Command period.

The entire faculty and staff of the School of Advanced Air and Space Studies (SAASS), Air University, Maxwell AFB, Alabama, have been supportive of this project. The commandant, Col Thomas E. Griffith, provided papers pertaining to General Brett from his collection of historical documents. Dr. Harold R. Winton kindly put me in touch with the National Military Personnel Records Center, St. Louis, Missouri, and Ms. Sandra Smith supported my effort to obtain the records of General Brett and his brother, Col Morgan L. Brett, with her efficient and friendly competence. My fellow students, too, in intended and unintended ways, lent their aid and ardor to the completion of this document.

Of particular help were the staff members of the Air Force Historical Research Agency, Maxwell AFB, Alabama. Dr. Herman Wolk and Dr. Roger Miller of the Air Force History Office, Bolling AFB, Washington, DC, shared their time and insight; specifically, Dr. Miller provided enthusiastic and immediate assistance from his vast store of knowledge and seasoned historical judgment whenever I asked. Mr. Stephen B. Chun, Air University Library, Maxwell AFB, Alabama, applied his prodigious awareness of textual references to the project with appreciable effect. The archivists who spent their time working through the project with me were of the greatest help, especially Mr. James Zobel, MacArthur Memorial, Norfolk, Virginia; Ms. Diane B. Jacob, Preston Library, Virginia Military Institute, Lexington, Virginia; Mr. Phil Edwards, National Air and Space Museum, Washington, DC; and Mr. Eric Voelz, National Military Personnel Records Center. Their expertise and willingness to assist bought me countless hours of productive research.

Finally, I offer my everlasting gratitude to my witty and supportive wife, Lynae, and my very understanding sons.

Chapter 1

Introduction

Lt Gen George H. Brett was an early air service pilot who served in World War I and had great success in the Air Corps during the interwar years. One of the few Airmen promoted to general officer rank during that time period, by 1940, when he became the chief of the Air Corps he was second only to Gen Henry H. Arnold in rank. Unlike Arnold, however, and some of Brett's other contemporaries such as Gen George C. Kenney, Brett's World War II service did not gain him lasting fame or a fourth star. Indeed, he spent the victorious years of World War II in the quiet backwater of Panama, ultimately retiring in 1945. Although he was immediately recalled to active duty until 1946 to continue his command in Panama, he was not sought out by the men who were building what was to become the independent Air Force.

Brett's star was rising very fast when, as a major general, Arnold dispatched him to conduct lend-lease discussions with the British and to make a tour of Africa. This trip turned out much differently than Brett might have expected, however; and an appealing journey back to the England he had known during World War I turned into a nightmare of biting insects, sweltering Javanese jungles, and relentless Japanese air superiority. The bad news continued as Brett faced logistical difficulties and laissez-faire attitudes in Australia. Senior to every American in the Far East, with the exception of Gen Douglas A. MacArthur, Brett was tasked with the chore of preparing a dispirited Australia as a friendly base to supply another man's glorious drive to conquer the enemy.

This book examines how well Gen George Brett executed the duties he was assigned during his tour in the Far East. The examination will focus on the pitfalls he faced and how the USAF could avoid them in future situations. Was there any opportunity for General Brett to succeed? If so, why did he fail?

Leadership Criteria

Several criteria are used to pass judgment on these questions. First, Brett's leadership is assessed. This assessment is based on the leadership characteristics of Gen George C. Marshall as identified by Forrest C. Pogue, US Army historian.[1] Since Marshall was a mentor to Brett and a fellow graduate of the Virginia Military Institute (VMI), it seems fair to grade him by the same standards that seemed to guide Marshall. Pogue lists eight characteristics of Marshall's leadership: (1) great self-certainty borne of experience and self-discipline, (2) ability to learn, (3) sense of duty, (4) willingness to accept responsibility, (5) simplicity of spirit, (6) character in its broadest sense, (7) loyalty, and (8) compassion.[2] An examination of Brett's life and career yields clues about how well he measured up to these eight characteristics.

As his portrait becomes clearer in this book, an image of a general officer who reflected his friend Marshall in many ways emerges. Even so, Brett's experience and self-discipline may not have led to the kind of self-certainty Marshall wielded so successfully. Further, simplicity of spirit would be a tall order for any powerful man, and it is not certain in this examination that Brett achieved it. Finally, the question of loyalty is carefully explored. Ultimately, Brett was a strong leader; the context of his command is sought in an attempt to determine just how strong.

Combat Execution

In war, of course, leadership is not the only ingredient for success. Brett's performance immediately preceding and during World War II should also be evaluated. Such an evaluation should be based on an understanding of what Brett himself knew and believed. A judgment with the benefit of hindsight, while impossible to avoid, neglects the mental exercise of working through the problems Brett faced with the tools he had available. His tools were not the personnel, materiel, and aircraft at Brett's disposal during his wartime command. Rather, tools in this context refer to his ability to use the resources he had to effectively lengthen resistance to the Japanese onslaught. This judgment is buttressed by examining his appreciation of contemporary doctrine and his ability to innovate by capitalizing on friendly strengths and exploiting enemy weaknesses. Thus, the question of whether Brett was able to adapt his doctrinal preconceptions rapidly enough to maximize his combat effectiveness will serve as the foundation for an assessment of his success or failure.[3]

Between the wars the Air Force's predecessor organizations began to develop a rudimentary doctrine, but tension existed between an understanding of war as a Clausewitzian contest of politics by other means and a Jominian delineation of principles to assure success. Maj Gen James E. Fechet became chief of the Air Corps on 14 November 1927. He expressed the Clausewitzian orientation of many Airmen in the following words:

> The objective of war is to overcome the enemy's will to resist, and the defeat of his army, his fleet or the occupation of his territory is merely a means to this end and none of them is the true objective. If the true objective can be reached without the necessity of defeating or brushing aside the enemy force on the ground or water and the proper means furnished to subdue the enemy's will and bring the war to a close, the object of war can be obtained with less destruction and lasting after effects than has heretofore been the case. At present the Air Force provides the only means for such an accomplishment.[4]

Such language will sound very familiar to the Airmen of today, schooled in the idea of centers of gravity. This type of thinking, however, created a conflict with the principles of war published in the US War Department Training Regulation 10-5, *Doctrine, Principles, and Methods*, 23 December 1921.[5] Undeterred, Airmen went on proclaiming that airpower was simply different. As George Brett was maturing as a field grade officer, intellectual foment within the Air Corps led to a codification of an Air Force mission and the organization of General Headquarters (GHQ) Air Force. This mission was expressed in an exercise directive of June 1934, explaining that "the mission of the GHQ Air Force included bombardment of enemy establishments and installations beyond the range of artillery, pursuit action to counter enemy air operations, long-range reconnaissance, and attacks against critical targets in the battle area." Pursuit aviation was given the task of protecting bombardment and preventing the operation of hostile aviation over friendly territory. In other words, the modern missions of close air support, interdiction, reconnaissance, and air superiority were already well established in the 1930s.[6]

By the time Brett went on his mission to England, relatively mature doctrinal ideas had been widely circulated by airpower proponents at the Air Corps Tactical School. These ideas focused on the missions listed above and were well known to Brett's contemporaries. His ability to marshal his airpower resources to accomplish those missions effectively is the key to evaluating his performance. Despite the fact that grand strategic considerations placed the Pacific theater at a lower priority for supply and allocation, is it possible Brett could have used Air Force doctrine to gain air superiority, halt the Japanese advance, and begin to erode their great Asian Empire?[7] This question forms the basis of a standard of combat execution against which General Brett was found wanting. One must hasten to add, however, that the mitigating circumstances make such a broad statement very misleading indeed.

Notes

(All notes appear in shortened form. For full details, see the appropriate entry in the bibliography.)

1. Pogue, "George C. Marshall," 193.
2. Ibid.
3. Howard, "Military Science in an Age of Peace," 7.
4. Futrell, *Ideas, Concepts, Doctrine*, 62–63.
5. Ibid.
6. Ibid., 75–76.
7. Eisenhower, *Eisenhower at War*, 77 and 80.

Chapter 2

Early Life and Career

Biographies are but the clothes and buttons of the man—the biography of the man himself cannot be written.

—Mark Twain

An overview of Gen George Howard Brett's early life and career lays the foundation for a study of his brief experience in the crucible of combat in World War II's Pacific theater. Born in Cleveland, Ohio, in 1886, George Howard Brett was the second son of a very prominent local family. His father, William Howard Brett, is the subject of Linda A. Eastman's 1940 book, *Portrait of a Librarian*. Brett's father was determined to serve in the Civil War and enlisted at age 18, becoming a musician. In his unit's first action he quit that title and fought as a rifleman for the remainder of the war. He met Brett's mother, Alice L. Allen, in church. The two married in May 1879 and had four sons and a daughter.[1]

The Brett boys and their sister grew up in a quickly expanding city on the edge of Lake Erie. By 1890 waves of immigration had produced a population of 261,355 people, making it the 10th largest city in America and 600 times larger than it had been 30 years before. Although disease and crime started to become serious in the 1890s, opportunities were also present.[2] The burgeoning city was home to citizens interested in increasing the prominence of their town, and they invested in the public library. Appointing William Howard Brett librarian in 1880, the library steadily grew in quality under his energetic hand.[3] He was secure enough in his position as head of the municipal library to start a family, and the proud parents first welcomed Morgan L. Brett, then a few years later George Howard was born on 7 February 1886. Two younger brothers, William Howard and Allen followed, along with a sister, Edith Alice.[4]

Cleveland was a prosperous and exciting city, and young George Howard saw motorcars traveling the streets before he was 10 years old. The telephone and electric light were also

George H. Brett circa 1909

new, but readily available in Cleveland. Cleveland's theaters and arts were developing rapidly, and the public library became a community center under the leadership of Brett's father, who developed the ideas of shelves open to the public, a children's section, and branch libraries accessible to residents of far-flung parts of the city. He also acquired titles to assist immigrants in mastering English and citizenship.[5]

As he grew up, George Howard and his brothers were inspired by the patriotism of the time. It would have been unusual for them not to be influenced by the public service of their father, and they were probably very proud of his heroism in the Civil War. Their father was a man of exceptional character, insisting on as much perfection as possible but always giving the credit to others and always making people feel comfortable and valued.[6] With such a role model prominent in their lives, the three older boys all sought military service. Eldest brother Morgan joined the class of 1906 at West Point, and after graduation served for many years as an ordnance officer, retiring in 1932 as a colonel.[7]

George was also determined to go to West Point. Appointments to the US Military Academy were very difficult to come by, even for families as prominent as the Bretts. Having already attained a nomination for his oldest son, William Brett was unable to obtain one for his second son. As a consequence, George Brett moved to Virginia, staying with his father's friends. In frustration he quit high school and went to work, eventually getting into the VMI. Having gained some maturity from his experience as a workingman and also being a few years older than the other men in the corps of cadets, he accomplished the course of study quickly and with great success.[8]

Brett graduated with the VMI class of 1909, and was appointed a second lieutenant of the Philippine Scouts on 22 March 1910, serving in the Philippines for a year and a half.[9] While there, Brett saw frequent combat fighting Muslim rebels. The constabulary consisted of local enlisted troops and white officers. He was assigned the additional duty of unit photographer and historian, bequeathing a photo album depicting his adventures to his oldest daughter.[10] Lt Gen Rock Brett, Gen George Howard's son, recounted his father's early career in 1981:

My father was commissioned in the 2d Philippine Constabulary. When he got out of VMI, he couldn't get a Regular commission. There weren't any. This was in 1909, and the threat of war was not that imminent. He was commissioned in the 2d Constabulary, and his ultimate goal in life was to be a Regular officer in the United States Army. He got a lot of advice from a lot of people, and one of the things he was told, "Hey, the only place to go is the Coast Artillery. That is the wave of the future." At that time we were building up these great coastal batteries, such as the fortified islands and the Canal Zone and various gun batteries . . . so he

7

applied for the Coast Artillery, but he failed his physical. It was always a family joke, and he used to laugh about it like mad because he was . . . very color blind so they wouldn't take him in the Coast Artillery. But he was sponsored by the US 2d Cavalry, which was at Fort Bliss. They were kind of the parent of the US Philippine Constabulary in the British tradition where you seconded your officers. So he had to wait. He laughs about that too. He said, "I had to wait for some idiot West Pointer to die." He claims that some West Pointer got drunk one night and fell off the balcony and broke his neck and they needed a cavalryman in a hurry so he was selected.[11]

Joining the Second Cavalry at Augur Barracks, Philippines, Brett returned to the United States in May 1912, stationed first at Fort Bliss, Texas, then starting in December 1913 at Fort Ethan Allen, Vermont.[12] It was during his stay in Vermont that Brett made connections that persisted throughout his career and life. He became fast friends with a fellow lieutenant of the Second Cavalry, Frank M. Andrews. Andrews was engaged to the daughter of Brig Gen James Allen. While standing up for Andrews as groomsman, Brett met one of the bridesmaids, the daughter of another Army man, Maj Gen Carroll L. Devol.[13] Brett married this young lady, Mary Devol, in Denver on 1 March 1916.[14]

Because Brett had volunteered to become an aviator when he was still a bachelor, General Devol was unwilling to countenance the marriage. He branded Brett a daredevil, and Brett and Mary had their nuptials at a friend's house, with only a distant Devol relation in attendance. The enmity did not last and Brett eventually became close to Mary's family.[15] In October 1915 he attended aviation school until August of the following year, when he graduated and was assigned to Washington, DC, in the office of the Chief Signal Officer.[16] His tour in Washington was graced by the birth of a daughter in 1917.[17] During that time he also served at Mineola, Long Island, New York. As war clouds developed over Europe, Brett's career continued to progress. He was promoted to first lieutenant in 1916 and to captain in 1917. In November of 1917 he left the United States bound for the glory of aerial combat in World War I.[18]

This dream was not realized. Fate intervened when the young captain suffered an appendicitis. Undergoing what was a dangerous operation in 1917, Brett was forced to spend much of his time recovering. Rock Brett recalls, "In those days when you had appendicitis, they cut you from belly button to backbone, and he was really incapacitated for quite a spell." He was removed from flying status, but this twist of fate put him in close contact with Brig Gen William "Billy" Mitchell, the ranking US Airman in France. Brett became Mitchell's senior materiel officer and eventually one of his die-hard supporters. Brett was objective about Mitchell, however, and considered him to be "moving too fast and that Billy Mitchell really—he had a great ego, and he was flamboyant. Sometimes he didn't do his homework too well." Nonetheless, Brett considered himself part of Mitchell's core of support. Rock Brett recalls, "I guess you could say they were a Mafia in one way, but they were all working the problem because they were all absolutely dedicated, convinced, and this was a fervent labor of—well, a lot more than love."[19]

As a materiel officer Brett spent a lot of time in England, but he also returned to Washington, DC, during the war to serve temporarily in the Office of the Director of Military Aeronautics. He worked there from 1 August to 23 September 1918, when he returned to England to take command of the Air Service Camp at Codford. He was responsible for the embarkation of Air Service troops there.[20] World War I was not all drudgery for Brett. While stationed in France he lived at the chateau of a very wealthy French woman with about nine other Americans. One of them was an ambulance driver named Cole Porter, who entertained his fellow residents with piano music when the men were off duty.[21]

At the close of the war Brett was a temporary major and listed among officers who had received a higher aeronautical rating than Reserve Military Aviator (RMA), and he was cited as a Junior Military Aviator (JMA) "prior to the armistice."[22] Fortunate enough to be assigned a command billet after the war, Brett made his way to Kelly Field, Texas, in December 1918. He commanded the aviation general supply depot until February 1919, when he became the maintenance and supply officer at the Air Service Flying School.[23]

Supply was a significant mission at Kelly, and Brett took over from Maj R. F. Scott, who had built the supply organization from scratch to accommodate the Mexican Punitive Expedition property arriving at Kelly Field. By the time Brett arrived, the supply department counted eight warehouses, 23 officers, and up to 1,700 enlisted members for temporary duties, as well as assets of $20 million. The local air service periodical of 27 February 1919, *The Kelly Field Eagle*, announced in the Pass in Review section, "Maj George F. Brott [*sic*] reported at this station and has been assigned to duty as air service supply officer." Brett is later celebrated with a quarter page photograph on the cover of the publication (name spelled correctly this time) noting the "many improvements" instituted since his assumption of command.[24]

Brett's evaluation record shows he had difficulty disciplining himself to salute smartly when the commander made a decision. In the summer of 1918 Col Halsey Dunwoody of the Air Service rated Brett "very good," but remarked that he was "somewhat given to forcing his own opinions." In a later appraisal Brett received a stinging rebuke from Col C. G. Edgar of the Air Service. Writing in the summer of 1919 Edgar evaluated Brett's service at the Kelly Field Supply Depot in the following words:

> This officer is not physically fit for service in the U.S. Army under War conditions either in the field or bureau work. During a visit to Washington on official business, while he was on duty with the Air Service in England, Major Brett was in my opinion head-strong and difficult to handle. His desires seemed to be more in securing leave of absence than to be helpful to the Washington office and the winning of the War.

> Much of the data and information that the Supply Section of the Air Service should have had in Washington in connection with the Handley-Paige [*sic*] product was in my opinion delayed in consequence thereto. Personally Major Brett is a very attractive and polished gentleman.[25]

In July 1919 he had a short tour at Fort Sam Houston, Texas, moving in October 1919 to command the Air Service depot at Morrison, Virginia, for one month. Next, he was assigned to the office of the director of the Air Service in Washington, DC. While there he became a permanent major in 1920.[26] He and Mary were blessed with a second daughter in that year.[27] His next step was to take command of Crissy Field, San Francisco, California. At the Presidio of San Francisco's Letterman General Hospital, his first son, future USAF Lt Gen Devol "Rock" Brett, was born.[28]

Command at Crissy Field was a choice assignment, and Brett had been preceded in command by the Air Force's future five-star general, Henry H. Arnold. In a post–World War I visit around the time of Brett's assumption of command, Marshal

Ferdinand Foch had declared Crissy Field to be the "last word" in airfields. During Brett's time Crissy Field's mission focused on coast artillery support:

> Aerial operations at Crissy Field consisted primarily of observation of artillery fire for the Coast Defenses of San Francisco; aerial photography; liaison flights for headquarters personnel; special civilian cooperation missions, such as search-and-rescue and publicity flights; and support for the U.S. Air Mail Service. The first Western aerial forest fire patrols were undertaken by Crissy Field pilots.[29]

The search and rescue aspect of Crissy Field's mission led to an interesting insight into Brett's command style and philosophy. The Crissy Field pilots deployed to San Diego, California, to conduct a search for Col Francis C. Marshall and Lt Charles C. Weber. Their deployment and search and rescue cross-country operations were led and evaluated by Brett. In response to a 15 January 1923 request by the chief of the Air Service to report on pilots qualified for cross-country flights, Brett sent reports on each of the pilots who participated in the mission. The cover letter is dated 24 February 1923. Brett rated eight pilots in addition to himself, giving each one an "above average" or better rating. He rated himself as "average" due to his lack of experience, but specified that his own judgment was "above average." By contrast, Maj Carl A. Spaatz's report from Self-ridge Field, Michigan, dated 5 February 1923, rated 18 pilots. He evaluated six as average, one below average, and the rest received higher ratings. He listed himself, but does not include an evaluation. Similarly, Maj Henry H. Arnold, in command at Rockwell Field, San Diego, California, rated five pilots (not including him), listing one as "about average;" the rest received higher ratings. Maj Ralph Royce, who later served as Brett's deputy in Australia, submitted the same report from his command at Brooks Field, Texas, on 1 February 1923. Rating 34 pilots, he graded 13 average, five below average, and the remainder receiving higher ratings. He did not list himself in the report.[30]

There are many reasons Brett may have delayed submitting his report for nearly a month after his fellow commanders did. Since he does not list the dates of the San Diego deployment, it might be assumed he filed the report when the fliers returned to Crissy Field. What is interesting, however, is Brett's hesitance to rate any of his pilots less than above average. If his rating of himself is to be taken at face value, roughly 10 percent of his pilots would be average or worse, although one suspects that an experienced flier like Brett was underrating his true abilities out of modesty. Royce rates half his pilots as average or worse, Spaatz rates 40 percent of his pilots as average or worse, and 20 percent of Arnold's small contingent is labeled average. Unless an unusually talented group of aviators had been assembled under Brett's command, which is certainly possible, it appears his evaluations were less strict than those of his contemporaries.[31]

In 1924 Brett left his command at Crissy Field and moved to the intermediate depot at Fairfield, Ohio, where he was officer in charge of the field service section, remaining in this post until 1927.[32] His duties are illustrated by a response he sent to the chief of the supply division in the Office of the Chief of the Air Service on 26 February 1926:

> With reference to basic memorandum of February 20, 1926 regarding emergency supplies for transient pilots along the Southern Airways Route, you are advised that this matter has been taken up with the San Antonio Depot and Commanding Officer, Biggs Field, with a view of making available such supplies as transient pilots may require in order that avoidable delays will not occur. Geo. H. Brett, Major, A.S., Chief of Section.[33]

Brett's days in the field were about to end, starting in June 1927 as he began the courses of instruction at the Air Corps Tactical School at Langley Field, Virginia. After the yearlong course, he was selected for the two-year Command and General Staff School at Fort Leavenworth, Kansas.[34]

Gen Rock Brett was old enough to recall his father's first tour at Fort Leavenworth. The school was extremely demanding, and Mary Brett continually found herself gently quieting the children to avoid disturbing her husband. The pressure increased when the Air Corps instructor at the school suddenly died, and Brett was appointed to take his place, simultaneously teaching and studying. Life had consolations, however, as the Brett family was neighbors with their close friends, the Frank M. Andrews family, and they enjoyed life on an Army Post.[35]

In the summer of 1930 Major Brett took command of Selfridge Field, Michigan, home of the famous First Pursuit Group, serving there until 1933. Among his many protégés was a brilliant young aviator named Curtis E. LeMay.[36] During the height of the great depression Brett was sensitive to the fact that, in contrast to the hardships faced by many other citizens; Army life was very good indeed. As the base commander and First Pursuit Group commander at Selfridge, Brett was able to care for the people under his command by providing mess facilities supported by an Army garden. He took care to remind the children how fortunate they were, showing them the effects of the depression on the civilians that lived near them. Although not a religious man, he strictly adhered to the promise he made to his Catholic wife to raise his children as Catholics, and he urged them to pray for Pres. Herbert Hoover. Brett was not politically motivated; however, as an Army officer he "had [his] hands full with the Army politics."[37]

Brett was the disciplinarian of the household. His son polished his father's boots and keenly remembers the Sam Browne belt that Brett always wore. Though he changed out of uniform when he came home for dinner, he wore a coat and a bow tie. Things were not always stern, as Brett relaxed with camping trips to a nearby spot known as Cranberry Lake. Even when they were camping, Rock Brett observes that his father was never profane—he, like his fellow officers, was a Victorian gentleman. A happy time of family togetherness was to last through a few more years of instructor duty and schooling, even as George Brett's Army career began to gather steam.[38]

Notes

1. Kent and Lancour, eds., *Encyclopedia of Library and Information Science*, 260–61.
2. Rose, *Cleveland*, 500.
3. Eastman, *Portrait of a Librarian*, 13–14.
4. Kent and Lancour, eds., *Encyclopedia of Library and Information Science*, 260–61.
5. Rose, *Cleveland*, 500.
6. Eastman, *Portrait of a Librarian*, 44–47.
7. Cullum, *Biographical Register of the Officers and Graduates of the U.S. Military Academy at West Point*.
8. Brett, oral history interview, 7. Brett's record card from the Virginia Military Institute (VMI) archives gives his standing as 19 of 40, right in the middle of his class. VMI Archives.

9. *Generals of the Army and the Air Force*, 2–3.

10. Devol Brett, interview.

11. Brett, oral history interview, 21.

12. *Generals of the Army and the Air Force*, 2–3.

13. Brett, oral history interview, 13–14.

14. *National Cyclopaedia of American Biography*, 54.

15. Brett, interviewed by author.

16. *Generals of the Army and the Air Force*, 2–3.

17. Brett, interviewed by author.

18. *National Cyclopaedia of American Biography*, 54.

19. Brett, oral history interview, 23–24. George H. Brett's medical record indicates his appendectomy occurred at Fort Bliss, Texas, in 1913, but that he underwent a kidney stone operation at Walter Reed Army Hospital, Washington, DC in 1917; and US Veterans Administration, VA Form 3101: *Request for Information, Brett, George H.*, 13 March 1958.

20. *Generals of the Army and the Air Force*, 2–3; and Brett, interview by the author. According to General Brett his father attained the rank of brevet lieutenant colonel during World War I.

21. Brett, interview by the author.

22. Air Service memorandum, subj: *Regular and Emergency Officers who received ratings above R.M.A. prior to the Armistice*, n.d., Record Group (RG) 18, box 290. The Reserve Military Aviator (RMA) rating required a significant demonstration of piloting skill, as described in letters from Lt William Muir Russel, a fallen World War I aviator: "Today, the last of my R.M.A. tests was successfully completed. This makes me a Reserve Military Aviator. The final tests are extended during three days. First, we were required to climb to an altitude of four thousand feet and remain there forty-five minutes. On the descent, we had to make one spiral to the right and one to the left with the motor shut down. The drop into the field was made with a dead engine from a height of one thousand feet, and the landing within two hundred feet of a designated mark. This is not the most dangerous, but by far the hardest to do accurately. The next was a triangular cross-country flight, covering a distance of sixty miles without a stop. Then, there were three tests, consisting of climbing to an altitude of five hundred feet without going out of the boundaries of a tract two thousand feet square. This is the most dangerous, because one is apt to get into a tail spin on the turns, which is very perilous if you are near the ground. Next, on landing, we had to jump a hurdle fifteen feet high, and land on the other side, coming to a stop within fifteen hundred feet of the hurdle; and last of all, a hundred mile cross-country flight without a stop. I am informed now that I am entitled to a commission, but it may be some time before it comes. It seems to take longer in the aviation than in the other branches of service." John Wheat, "Contribution from John Wheat—Learning to Fly in the AEF." The Junior Military Aviator was a rating authorized by Congress on 18 July 1914, the Military Aviator rating was a certificate issued to officers before passage of that act. Brett received his Junior Military Aviator Rating on 2 September 1916.

23. *National Cyclopaedia of American Biography*, 54.

24. The Stratemeyer Papers.

25. Department of Defense (DOD), *Efficiency Report, George H. Brett*, (Paris: General Headquarters American Expeditionary Force, Summer 1918), n.p.; DOD, *Efficiency Report, George H. Brett* (Detroit, MI: Commanding Officer, August 1919), n.p. Edgar's discontent with Brett's physical fitness is difficult to understand, unless the young Airman was still suffering from the kidney problems that plagued him in 1917. As for Brett's anxiety about leave, it is possible this was related to his father's accidental death, which occurred on 24 August 1918. He could well have had urgent family business to transact.

26. *National Cyclopaedia of American Biography*, 54. A memorandum at National Archives II indicates there were only 122 majors in the Air Service as of fall 1919; Air Service Memorandum, Central Decimal Files 1917–1938, Air Corps Officers, file group 211, RG 18, box 290.

27. Brett, interviewed by author.

28. Brett, oral history interview, 12.

29. Haller, "Aviation at Crissy Field."

30. RG 18, Cross-Country Flying Reports, box 296.

31. Ibid.

32. *National Cyclopaedia of American Biography*, 54.

33. RG 18, Memorandum, 26 February 1926, box 296.

34. *Generals of the Army and the Air Force*, 2–3.

35. Brett, oral history interview, 37.

36. Brett, interview by the author.

37. Brett, oral history interview, 35–36.

38. Ibid., 36–39.

Chapter 3

The Buildup to War

When his tour at Selfridge was over, Brett became the Air Corps instructor at Fort Leavenworth, Kansas, from 1933 to 1935.[1] He regarded this as a golden opportunity to undo some of the division he felt had been created by Mitchell and attempted to reach out to ground officers. With the help of the few aviators in the class at Fort Leavenworth, Brett tried to make other Army officers understand the importance of airpower and its value as a supporting arm to the ground forces. According to Rock Brett there was no agreed-upon program to proselytize for airpower among the men of the Air Corps, but as true believers they spontaneously tried to educate anyone who would listen.[2] After nearly 16 years as a major, Brett was finally promoted to lieutenant colonel and selected to attend the Army War College, Carlisle, Pennsylvania.[3]

At the Army War College Brett worked hard and became a student leader for the Gettysburg Campaign study. Nervous about doing a good job teaching his classmates, he used his son to refine his lecture:

> He said, "If you understand this—and at that time I was going to Gordon Junior High School, and I was in about the fifth or sixth grade—those blankety-blank Army guys will understand it. Now if you don't understand, tell me." He used me as his pupil. Then he went up there, and at that time the commandant of the Army War College was a colonel, and my father was selected to be commander of the 19th Wing in the Panama Canal Zone, which was one of the very few general officer slots in the Army Air Corps and one that was just really neat. This commandant, before my father started his presentation, said, "I have some very good news but, frankly, very humbling news," words to this effect. . . . "To introduce to you, soon-to-be, Brigadier General George H. Brett." It was a brevet rank. So that was the first word that he got because they were very close hold about this. And of course, that really made the day. We went to Panama, and he was a BG."[4]

Brett had no idea at the time, but his command in Panama prepared him for a more difficult assignment later in his career. His wife, who had attended Catholic schools in Baltimore, knew many of the wealthy Central and South American families through their daughters, who had been her classmates. This valuable entrée into Latin American society helped the Bretts to have a very successful tour. As much a political as a military representative, Brett and his family traveled extensively throughout Central and South America. In the process Brett came to understand the area, its geopolitical structure, and its military vulnerabilities.[5]

Brett apparently had some work to do when he arrived in Panama. A memorandum prepared by General Brett's executive officer on 22 May 1937 gave two pages worth of rules for items to be routed through General Brett and indicated slipshod procedures of the past were to be rectified. On 11 October 1937 Brett sent a request to his staff to prepare briefing items for him to take to a conference in Washington, but the request caught them by surprise. The recipient of the request noted, "keep such things as I can think of from time to time to be quickly rounded up when called for. Have Col L., Maj P., Capt C., [illegible] read this letter. They may have something."[6]

Brett's work in Panama received mixed reviews, beginning with his first general officer efficiency report on 9 January 1937. Brett started out strong, rating seven of 27 brigadiers known to Maj Gen H. W. Butner. From there, however, his performance fluctuated dramatically. In April 1937 Gen F. W. Rowell rated him five of 18; in July 1937 Gen David L. Stone rated him 10 of 39; but in March 1938 Stone's appraisal plunged to 21 of 25. General F. H. Smith rated him as 24 of 36 in April 1938, after over a year in command. Rated again by General Stone in July 1938, Brett improved again and he ranked 12 of 45. By September 1938 Stone ranked him 10 of 41, calling him "an enthusiastic officer with zeal and initiative and capacity for handling men."[7]

While the Bretts were in Panama, their children were growing up and leaving home. The oldest daughter, Dora, fell in love with Bernard A. Schriever, Brett's aide; and the two were married in General Arnold's home. According to Maj Gen Howard C. Davidson, Brett telegraphed Arnold to ask him to look after Schriever. Davidson recalled, "We had to put on this marriage for them, which we did, for Brett. Arnold dumped a lot of that on me."[8] Schriever took young Rock Brett for a number of airplane rides, as did General Brett. Rock recalls that Schriever let him have more fun in the air than his father did.[9]

Dora's wedding to Schriever occurred shortly after the death of Maj Gen Oscar Westover, who "ran the Air Force from his hip pocket. There were so many things happening that General Arnold, who was his deputy, didn't really know." When he died Brett felt as though his career had become very uncertain.[10] Replaced in Panama by Brig Gen H. A. Dargue, Brett had to return to being a lieutenant colonel.[11] Brett was briefly stationed in Menlo Park, California, where his son attended Palo Alto High School. It was a period of great upheaval in the Air Corps, and Brett was soon moved to Langley, Virginia, as chief of staff for his friend Frank M. Andrews.[12]

Andrews had taken command of the GHQ Air Force in March of 1935 and had surrounded himself with a capable staff of future general officers that included Harvey B. S. Burwell, Follett Bradley, George Kenney, and Joseph E. McNarney. Major Hugh Knerr was the chief of staff. Doing his best to implement the recommendations of the Drum Board, Andrews came into conflict with the Army chief of staff, General MacArthur. When private testimony to congressmen was leaked to the press, MacArthur surprised Andrews with a reprimand.[13] This incident led Brett to believe that his friendship with Andrews might have been the reason for his eventual conflict with MacArthur.[14] By 1938 Andrews' small contingent could credit themselves with some progress for airpower, despite the serious austerity of government financial support. In that year Brett joined the GHQ Air Force as the chief of staff.

Brett received a favorable rating from his old friend, Frank M. Andrews. Andrews said his performance as chief of staff, GHQ Air Force, was superior, while his performance as a military airplane pilot was excellent. Brett was downgraded from superior to excellent only in the qualifications of physical activity and endurance, but his medical record is mute about any health troubles he might have experienced during that time. Andrews wrote that Brett was "a very practical, forceful officer, who uses his head at all times."[15] He must have known that his friend Andrews had already turned down an offer from Army Chief of Staff general Malin Craig to succeed Westover. By 1 March 1939, Andrews had been sent to Fort Sam Houston as a colonel, his career temporarily on hold as punishment for refusal to cease advocating the B-17.[16]

Brett left GHQ Air Force at about the same time, reporting to Wright Field, Dayton, Ohio, as assistant to the chief of the Air Corps in February 1939. Detailed as commandant of the Air Corps Engineering School and the chief of the materiel division, Brett's fortunes, unlike his friend Andrews, had improved and he was once again a brigadier general.[17] The buildup for war was keeping his command very busy, and Brett took the time to explain some of the challenges he faced in a news article in the August 1940 edition of *Aviation*:

> The Air Corps is hopeful that the delays incident in the old system of procurement will now be eliminated and that negotiation will permit [sic] a continuation of the procurement of the various types of airplanes without interruption. It is recognized that approximately seven to nine months elapse before the airplanes developed from an experimental type previously supplied can be rolled out of the door and flown away.[18]

Brett goes on to give a detailed explanation of the procurement process, including industrial requirements like raw materials, various categories of labor, machine tools, transportation, gasoline, and miscellaneous equipment.[19] He continues with a description of airplane evaluation procedures and research and development. The vast scope of his responsibilities is evident from the discussion. Like his boss, General Arnold, he was also aware that the time to develop the industrial infrastructure the nation needed for wartime production was very limited.[20]

Slightly more than a month after his article was published in *Flying and Popular Aviation*, George Brett was promoted again, this time to major general, and became the acting chief of the Air Corps.[21] This title was transitory, and the status of senior Air Corps personnel was confused. Arnold refers to himself as chief of the Air Corps in a 7 February 1941 letter to Rock Brett about the Army's claim to ownership of Moffat Field, California.[22] Brett formally became chief of the Air Corps for a four-year term, beginning in May 1941.[23] In another article by Brett in September 1941 he illuminated the confusing organizational structure of the Army Air Forces (AAF). Brett explained that as chief of the Air Corps, he was subordinate to Arnold, chief of air forces and deputy chief of staff for air. A separate air organization, Combat Command, contained the fighting forces, while the Air Corps had four responsibilities: (1) training, (2) procurement and supply, (3) engineering, and (4) construction.[24]

The tone of this article was dramatically different than the procurement article in *Aviation*. While the previous discussion was almost stilted in its formality, in this article Brett used informal analogies and avidly described the enormity of the challenge faced by the Air Corps in discharging its mission. The end of the article is somewhat difficult to understand and bears repeating at length, as it seems to reveal a slightly put-upon attitude, perhaps engendered by Brett's long association with materiel:

> Suffice it to say in the short space afforded by the mechanical limitations of this particular article that the Air Corps has as many responsibilities, though on a huger scale, as a housewife.

> That is perhaps why the Air Corps has been referred to as the "housekeeping" Corps unit of the Army Air Forces. Possibly that is reasonably correct terminology, because the Air Corps, like the housekeeper, has heavy responsibilities, endless work, and little enough glory.

> This is quite as it should be, because the housewife is not looking for glory, neither is the Air Corps. The housewife has heavy demands made upon her by all members of the family, and she takes her satisfaction in keeping a roof over the heads of her family—feeding them, clothing them, seeing to it that they are properly schooled and made ready for their work in life.

> She may not be a glamor girl, and this pleases her because she does not desire to be a glamor girl; she would rather the members of her family turned to her with their problems, and their difficulties, and their emergencies than that she be glorified above and beyond her just desserts.

> There is little that is glamorous, little enough glorification, in most of the work of the Air Corps. It is for the most part just work, and then more work, and then still more work. As it grapples with its terrific job, with its heavy responsibilities, and solves some of its manifold problems and fails to solve others, only to start from scratch and try again, its back may be bent under the increasing load, but its heart is light.

> Its heart is light, because no matter what harder tasks the future may have in store, the Air Corps can say with Kipling: "After me cometh a builder tell him I, too, have known."[25]

Regardless of his feelings about his role as the chief of the Air Corps, Brett hardly could have been better suited to the task. Considering his experience from World War I forward in the world of supply and maintenance, he was the ideal officer to handle the impending industrial buildup for wartime aviation. His ratings for his work in the materiel division and as chief of the Air Corps did not place him above all his peers. General Arnold rated

Brett for his concurrent duties as chief, materiel division, and commandant of the Air Corps Engineering School in June 1939. Superior in all areas except endurance, in which he received an excellent, Arnold ranked him eight of 41. The next year, for the same duties, he was downgraded to excellent as commandant. His other ratings remained the same, while Arnold's overall ranking improved to five of 40. Arnold wrote in June of 1941 that Brett had performed in a superior manner as the assistant chief of the Air Corps, but "His personal views at times govern his course of action rather than willing and generous support to the plans of his superiors." Brett's rank remained five of 40.[26]

Before his *Flying and Popular Aviation* article was published, Brett was on his way to Great Britain to find out how the Air Corps could better support Royal Air Force (RAF) lend-lease requirements.[27] General Brett was not taking a direct route to England. In August Rock Brett remembers standing on the airfield with his mother, getting ready to bid goodbye to his father. His father asked him to climb the ladder up into the LB-30 that was one of three forming the formation that would pioneer a southern air route to the Middle East.[28] Once inside, Brett told his son: "I want to introduce you to a very special individual. This is Bombardier/Navigator/Pilot Captain LeMay. He will lead our formation through uncharted territory to resupply the Middle East." Brett then enjoined his son to take care of his mother. LeMay successfully led the formation first to Natal, Brazil, then across the southern Atlantic and through the African desert, arriving safely with all three aircraft in Cairo, Egypt, while avoiding areas where the Germans controlled the air. [29]

Between August and November of 1941 Brett worked with the various British agencies responsible for production and maintenance, recommending to General Arnold that American labor and facilities be established in England and Northern Ireland to handle the repair, assembly, and equipping of American aircraft. Brett's recommendations caused great concern in Washington, and Arnold's response prompted Brett to reassure him with the following cable:

> This is for Gen. Arnold. Reference your 417, my 819 was to impress upon you the persistence with which I am following up this subject. For the purpose of clearing up the situation as soon as possible, I again discussed the entire matter with Colonel Moore-Brabazon. The tremen-

dous demand upon all available facilities, equipment and personnel to meet your programs are thoroughly appreciated by me and I am making no commitments until I have presented the matter in detail to you for consideration in connection with your problems. Except for the recommendation for a small detachment to correlate supply systems and work with the R.A.F. Hq. Staff on detailed requirements, my No. 857 was purely a presentation of policy. This detail would live with the operational base Hq. of the R.A.F. installation in Northern Ireland and become acquainted thoroughly with any peculiarities of base and tactical operations. I have no peculiar ideas and I am not giving anything away without your specific approval. I repeat that I am not making any commitments and am exercising the greatest care to in no way commit you to action until the entire matter has been presented. BRETT [30]

Ultimately in cable number 498 General Arnold disapproved "any plan to take over all maintenance and repair of all R.A.F. operated American-built airplanes, due to the non-availability of air force personnel and equipment; approved negotiations for equipment and management of operation of depot in North Ireland."[31]

Brett's presence was causing concern to his hosts as well. On a visit to Air Marshal Sir Arthur Tedder in the Middle East on 10 September 1941, Brett impressed the British air commander as "a pleasant, quiet-spoken man," but Tedder soon concluded he would get little help from Brett on his pressing problems of resupply. Tedder remarked, ". . . so far as I could find out he was interested only in supply and maintenance." Brett's tendency to speak his mind seemed to Tedder to do more harm than good:

I thought Brett was anxious to help. . . . But before I had finished the letter in which I was reporting . . . to Portal, I learned that General Brett had somewhat antagonized [sic] the Minister of State by making some comments which were possibly too outspoken. By 23 September Sir Miles Lampson felt obliged to telegraph to [British Foreign Secretary Sir Anthony] Eden that he had seen Brett several times and that the General was so frankly critical that his comments ought to be passed on to the Foreign Office. Brett's first criticism, it appeared, was that a unified command should be set up. . . . Brett bitterly criticised the confusion and lack of efficient organization in Suez, where there were in his view too many separate authorities. . . .

I could not deny that by now the charms of General Brett's company were beginning to pall. After a talk with him on the afternoon of 25 September I wondered in my journal how he and all the American visitors could lay down the law about things of which they knew next to nothing. . . . Two days afterwards, I was told in a signal from the Air Ministry that [Royal Air Force Liaison Air Marshal Arthur] Bert Harris in Washington had reported a statement by Brett that my Chief Maintenance

> Officer, Dawson, was complaining bitterly of the lack of proportion in the allotment of spares . . . presumably by the Air Ministry. I . . . was requested to ensure that discretion was used in giving information to prominent American visitors. . . .
>
> I asked my informant to believe that neither Dawson nor I was in the habit of throwing mud at the Air Ministry. If Brett and his cohort were to help, they had to be given the facts, but I feared that no discretion on our part could ensure discretion by Brett and Harris. I observed that loose statements by the former which were passed on and lost nothing in the telling by the latter, seemed more likely to prejudice relations between the Middle East and the Air Ministry than those between the Air Ministry and the United States.[32]

Tedder was further concerned when he learned that Brett's mission to support the British air effort in the Middle East was tainted by Brett's agenda to foster an independent air arm in the US military establishment:

> I hoped, but without undue confidence, that Brett was not going to make trouble. I feared that he suffered from the apparently not uncommon American complaint of going off at half-cock with sweeping criticisms and proposals, and gathered from various sources that he was a leading light in the controversy about the Army Air Corps as opposed to the independent Air Force in the United States. A few days before, one of the American party had remarked to me that the Middle East was regarded as a laboratory for this controversy. Each American appeared to send back cables with snippets of information and opinion which suited his own particular school of thought, and I told the Air Ministry that everything Brett said had to be viewed in this light. Apart from this aspect, I still thought his views generally sound and practical. Of course, he had never before seen squadrons operating under real war conditions, and was, I thought, horrified at the working conditions and improvisations which were necessary.[33]

Brett remained focused on supply and maintenance issues, despite his interest in an independent air arm. In a letter of 22 November 1941 to Col Moore-Brabazon, the minister of aircraft production, Brett explained that a base depot could not be established in England, but that the War Department would establish a repair depot in Northern Ireland under cost-sharing terms he outlined in the document. He also stated he was returning to Washington via the Middle East, expecting to be back in his office by 15 December 1941.[34] Mars intervened, however, and General Brett's destiny was never to return to his office in Washington. The next time he was in Washington was August of 1942. Standing before his friend and fellow VMI graduate, Army Chief of Staff George C. Marshall on that summer day, George H. Brett had every expectation of facing a court-martial.[35]

Notes

1. *National Cyclopaedia of American Biography*, 54.
2. Brett, interview by the author.
3. *National Cyclopaedia of American Biography*, 54.
4. Brett, oral history interview, 46.
5. Brett, interview by the author.
6. RG 18, Memorandum, 11 October 1937, Panama Air Depot France Field, Canal Zone, 1933–1939, file group 000.4-300.4, box 2.
7. DOD, *Efficiency Reports, George H. Brett*, (Quarry Heights, Panama: Commanding General, January 1937–September 1938).
8. Green, "Prelude to Pearl Harbor Attack."
9. Brett, oral history interview, 48.
10. Ibid., 42.
11. RG 18, 18 August 1939, file group 000.4-300.4, item 312.
12. Brett, oral history interview, 43.
13. Copp, *Frank M. Andrews*, 11–14. MacArthur had been retained in the post of chief of staff for a fifth year by President Roosevelt; he departed for the Philippines in the fall of 1935. General of the Army Douglas MacArthur, *Reminicences*, 102–3.
14. Brett with Kofoed, "The MacArthur I Knew," 149.
15. DOD, *Efficiency Report, George H. Brett*, (Langley Field, VA: Commanding General, February 1939), 1–2.
16. Copp, *Frank M. Andrews*, 14. While there is no doubt Andrews' outspokenness had won him no friends in Washington, he nevertheless received a pivotal command assignment, so the "punishment" was not necessarily intended to damage his career. Miller to author, subject: Gen George Brett Thesis Questions, 16 April 2004.
17. *National Cyclopaedia of American Biography*, 54.
18. Brett, "Defense Procurements," 42–43 and 130.
19. He included nylon instead of silk for parachutes, flying clothing, and other textiles, optics, and specially processed paper for electrical windings. Brett, "Defense Procurements,"130.
20. Ibid., 134.
21. *National Cyclopaedia of American Biography*, 54.
22. Arnold, "Pre-War Correspondence."
23. *National Cyclopaedia of American Biography*, 54.
24. Brett, "US Army Air Corps," 67.
25. Ibid., 68 and 202.
26. DOD, *Efficiency Reports, George H. Brett* (Washington, DC: Chief of the Air Corps, June 1939–June 1941).
27. Arnold, "Brett Mission to England."

28. In March 1941 the British received six of the YB-24 prototypes, which were redesignated "Liberator British 30" or LB-30 for short. "Consolidated LB30."

29. Brett, interview by the author.

30. Arnold, "Brett Mission to England."

31. Ibid.

32. Tedder, *With Prejudice*, 159–61.

33. Ibid., 161.

34. Arnold, "Brett Mission to England."

35. Brett, interview by the author.

Chapter 4

Conflagration in the Pacific

Far to the west, General MacArthur knew the Japanese were going to invade the Philippines. What he did not know was when. MacArthur, the target of George Brett's postwar recriminations, made his home in the Philippines after his term as Army chief of staff ended on 18 September 1935. There he served as military adviser to Philippine president Manuel Quezon.[1] Throughout the remainder of the 1930s MacArthur made plans to defend against the anticipated Japanese attack, but received little support from Washington, DC, until he wrote directly to the Chief of Staff general George C. Marshall, in February 1941. Asking for an augmentation of War Department plans to defend the entire Philippine archipelago, MacArthur won Marshall's qualified support for a military buildup. By July 1941 War Department policy shifted to contemplate the dedication of men and equipment to the Philippines. The reinforcement of the US Far Eastern possession started too late. Publicly, MacArthur announced the Japanese would not strike until after April 1942. Army estimates predicted a surprise attack in the winter months, and planners envisioned an invasion force of 100,000 enemy troops.[2]

As the US forces in the Philippines scrambled to prepare for war, Gen George Brett was flying in the opposite direction. A letter of instructions, dated 19 August 1941, directed Brett to look into: (1) maintenance of American planes in England; (2) repair of equipment at Singapore; Basra; Port Sudan, Sudan; Cairo, Egypt; Takoradi, Ghana; Northern Ireland; and England; (3) ferrying of equipment across the Atlantic; and (4) radio operator and mechanic training in the United Kingdom.[3] Brett's experience in supply and materiel made him the perfect man for this job, but Gen Ira C. Eaker reflected 15 years later that Arnold may have sent Brett on a long trip to get him out of the way. According to Eaker, Arnold was disappointed in Brett's performance as chief of the Air Corps: "Brett tended to be a little bit contentious. Arnold would tell him something to do, and he would argue about it. So Arnold replaced him very shortly and sent him overseas, down to Australia." Eaker observed that although Arnold wanted someone more responsive, progressive, and dynamic, Brett and Arnold "remained to the end, so far as I know, very close personal friends, but at that time, with the pressure that was on Arnold, Arnold had to measure a man not by personal likes and dislikes, but by the man's ability to do the job."[4]

Visiting London, Gibraltar, and Malta throughout the autumn of 1941, Brett was working to eliminate supply bottlenecks for both the British and the Russians, as well as to report on British air units at war.[5] His primary base of operations was Cairo. According to an anecdote in the Roanoke, Virginia, newspaper, he became the first American general to be shot at in World War II when his British bomber was fired upon by an Axis destroyer.[6] By the winter of 1941 Brett was preparing to return to the United States; at his Cairo farewell party he received a telegram from Washington, DC, ordering him to proceed to Chungking, China.[7] Brett presumed this order was prompted by the 7 December 1941 attack on Pearl Harbor.[8]

In November General Brett had cabled the War Department requesting an airplane be sent to Cairo to return him to the United States since his mission was completed. An aircrew was dispatched from Headquarters AAF for Brett's return trip. According to Brig Gen Edward H. Alexander:

> The Nips did their Dec [ember] 7th thing at Honolulu, and I had packed to go over for two weeks and bring General Brett back to the US. I didn't get back until 1943. We got into the war. So, from November 1941 until I got back in Oct 1943, I was in China, Burma and India, completely out of touch with AF Hqs., excepting by radio communications.
>
> [Interviewer] Did you go to Delhi?
>
> [Alexander] No, we went to Rangoon, Burma. . . . We talked with Chennault. . . . The first thing I did when I got on the ground there at Mingleadon [AB in Rangoon] was go to the RAF photo section and ask them if they had any fresh photos of Bangkok. They had. They were washing them; [the photos] were wet. This officer pulled one out and said 'Here.' And I started to count, and I got over 100 airplanes—just over here at Bangkok. I got hold of Brett and said we'd better get his airplane out of there. He said I couldn't go. We sent the copilot without an assistant and a crew and got the airplane to Calcutta. Two nights later, the Nips came over and bombed the place.[9]

After 10 days in Rangoon, Burma, Brett departed for Chung-king to visit Generalissimo Chiang Kai-shek, presumably in the company of British general Archibald Wavell, recently transferred from combat command in the Middle East.[10] Chiang offered Wavell Chinese troops for the defense of Burma, which the English general reluctantly accepted.[11] Brett participated in conferences in Chungking and Rangoon before departing China for Australia on 24 December 1941.[12]

The eventful first weeks of the war in the Pacific were taking their grim toll on the men who were falling back in the face of the relentless Japanese advance. While Brett was traveling from Cairo and conferring with Wavell and Chiang, MacArthur's contingent of fighters and bombers was being crushed by Japanese airpower.[13] Maj Gen Lewis H. Brereton, the ranking Airman in the Philippines, requested permission to move his battered headquarters south after two weeks of disastrous defeat. This request was granted on 23 December 1941.[14]

About the same time Brett was having his own combat adventures, as reported in an enthusiastic wartime narrative of his exploits:

> Near Rangoon, a flight of 71 Japs got on the tail of [Wavell and Brett's] Douglas transport. At Mingalodon in Burma, they landed on a friendly airdrome, dived into a trench. Bombs, shrapnel, machine-gun slugs, were falling as thickly around them as snowflakes. . . . Three hundred "heavies" exploded on that field. The Japs played hard for their chance to knock out the whole Supreme Command at once. Thumpers came as close as 20 yards; dive bombers stitched the trench with machine-gun sprays. But neither general was hurt, although both got plenty muddied.
>
> With as much aplomb as can be mustered, when your elbows and knees are in each other's face, and the din is hellish, Wavell and Brett talked shop in the trench, to the undying admiration of their aides; then calmly went indoors to continue the conference when the Japs had been chased off by the R.A.F and the American Volunteer Group.[15]

Command arrangements were confused and frequently changed during December 1941. On 13 December 1941 Brig Gen Julian Barnes was aboard a reinforcement convoy bound from Honolulu to the Philippines when he received word that his command had been redirected to Australia. Further, he learned he was appointed overall US commander, United States Army Forces in Australia (USAFIA). For about a week, Barnes held this command, but on 21 December 1941 he was informed by message

29

that Gen George Brett would be assigned to "organize and command all American units." Barnes was only one day away from Australia—his convoy arrived 22 December 1941.[16]

Two days later Brett departed Chungking for Australia, but his role as the commanding general of USAFIA was made somewhat ambiguous by his concurrent assignment as deputy commander for the coalescing American, British, Dutch, and Australian Command (ABDACOM). Wavell was selected as ABDA's supreme commander on 29 December 1941.[17] This was formalized between Pres. Franklin Roosevelt and British Prime Minister Winston Churchill by correspondence shortly after New Year's, 1942. A draft presidential announcement dated 3 January 1942 describes the basic concept of unified command for the Southwest Pacific area:

1. As a result of the proposals put forward by the American and British Chiefs of Staff, and of their recommendations to President Roosevelt and to the Prime Minister, Mr. Churchill, it is announced that, with the concurrence of the Netherlands Government and of the Dominion Governments concerned, a system of unified Command will be established in the South West Pacific Area.

2. All the forces in this area, sea, land and air, will operate under one Supreme Commander. At the suggestion of the President, in which all concerned have agreed, General Sir A. Wavell has been appointed to this Command.

3. Major-General George H. Brett, Chief of the Air Corps of the U.S. Army, will be appointed Deputy Supreme Commander. He is now in the Far East. Under the direction of General Wavell, Admiral Thomas C. Hart, U.S. Navy, will assume Command of all naval forces in the area. General Sir Henry Pownall will be Chief of Staff to General Wavell.

4. General Wavell will assume his Command in the near future.[18]

The Allies bound together by ABDACOM had very different strategic goals. While the Americans hoped to relieve the Philippines and delay the Japanese advance toward Australia long enough to establish a base of operations there, the British were focused primarily on preventing the fall of Singapore. The Dutch, on the other hand, were primarily concerned with the preservation of the Netherlands East Indies (NEI).[19] Since Holland had already been occupied by Germany, the Dutch forces in the Pacific were fighting for their independence, as well as for their homes. The Australians, like the Americans, were keen to prevent the Japanese from invading their continent. Australian interests conflicted with those of the United States when it came to supplies from America. The Australians did not want to see war materiel diverted to the Philippines or NEI that could be built up in Australia to resist the anticipated Japanese invasion.[20]

ABDACOM's naval component attempted to combine the Dutch Pacific fleet with US naval forces originally based in the Philippines. Poorly trained and equipped ground forces were provided by the British and Dutch and to a limited extent the United States. The Australians provided goodwill and a small number of ships and aircraft. Land forces fell to the Dutch, under the command of Lt-Gen Hein ter Poorten and his British deputy. Most of the air forces were US planes and crews that escaped death and destruction in the Philippines during the month of December. They were commanded by Air Marshal Sir Richard Pierse of the United Kingdom, but Lt Gen Lewis H. Brereton, his deputy, held command until Pierse's arrival.[21] Brett sent a message to MacArthur on 1 February 1942 explaining the ABDACOM arrangements:

> FOR MACARTHUR FROM BRETT [.] MY HEADQUARTERS [:] ABDA-COM [,] LOEMBANG N E I [.] AS DEPUTY C IN C HAVE GENERAL OVERALL CONTROL OVER SERVICE OF SUPPLY [,] U S ARMED FORCES IN AUSTRALIA [.] BRERETON COMMANDING U S AIR FORCES ABDA AREA [,] HEADQUARTERS ABDACOM [.] HEADQUARTERS U S ARMED FORCES IN AUSTRALIA [,] MELBOURNE GENERAL BARNES COMMANDING [.] DARWIN IS HEADQUARTERS BASE NUMBER ONE [,] U S ARMED FORCES IN AUSTRALIA AND IS ONLY A TRANSSHIP-MENT POINT FROM AUSTRALIA TO N E I [.] COL LA RUE COMMAND-ING [.] ALL COMMUNICATIONS SHOULD BE ADDRESSED TO ABDA-COM REPEAT TO USAFIA MELBOURNE [.] BRETT[22]

General Brett spent the beginning of January in Darwin, Australia, where he was struggling to organize the AAF and Allied operations there. On 5 January 1942 Brett called Arnold and begged him for instructions over a very poor telephone connection. Brett reported that he would meet with General Wavell in two days and requested specifics about how to conduct US-Australian operations. Arnold promised instructions would be cabled and asked Brett if he had a code book, to which Brett replied he had no code book with him in Darwin. The message would have to be sent through the military attaché in Melbourne.[23]

31

The difficult communications further stymied poor coalition co-ordination, and to make things worse the various ABDACOM components were geographically separated. General Brett and General Wavell conducted business from the Grand Hotel, Lembang, Java; the naval component of ABDACOM was also head-quartered there. Brereton had his headquarters in Baedong, Java, roughly 25 kilometers away. Key naval staff and logistics were over 400 miles from Lembang in Surabaya, Java. Naval resupply was from Darwin, Australia, 1,200 miles from the NEI.[24]

Even as Wavell and Brett were establishing their headquarters in Lembang, it was becoming clear to planners in Washington, DC, that it would be very difficult to challenge Japanese air superiority in the region. At the end of January, Gen Dwight D. Eisenhower advised General Marshall in a handwritten memorandum that US participation in ABDACOM should be limited to AAF and associated ground support. On 22 January Brett called Arnold by phone to "energetically" request high-ranking air officers for the Far East, as well as additional aircraft. Experienced leadership was needed, and rank was important because the British had filled out the ABDACOM staff with numerous generals. Brett asked permission to commission some men and promote officers; Arnold assured Brett that he already had that authority. Apparently Brett was not receiving all of Arnold's cables. In a 28 January letter Brett reiterated his plea for more high-ranking personnel, admitting he was losing track of details.[25]

Allied air force morale was low in the NEI, and although 60 bombing missions were mounted during ABDACOM's short existence, difficult operating conditions, inexperience, and Japanese air superiority all contributed to a high attrition rate. Lack of discipline and a helpless, lackadaisical attitude among AAF officers were noted by Generals Brett and Brereton at the end of January 1942.[26] By 1 February 1942 Eisenhower had concluded in Washington, DC, that Japanese successes in Sumatra had made it impossible to move B-17s from Bangalore, India, to airfields in Java.[27]

Events began to deteriorate very rapidly for ABDACOM in the first months of 1942, as fortune continued to smile upon the empire of Japan. Wavell formally assumed command on 15 January 1942, and the next day Japan began its invasion of

Figure 1. Eastern NEI map

Burma.[28] A British possession, Burma had just been transferred from India to the ABDACOM theater. Wavell's attention
was almost entirely diverted by his duties in the NEI, although
he flew the 2,000 miles to Burma twice during the next five
weeks.[29] President Roosevelt and Prime Minister Churchill consolidated the command arrangements the Australians and the
Dutch were required to accept at the beginning of February
1942, formalized by a letter from Churchill to Roosevelt:

33

[SECRET] AND PERSONAL TO THE PRESIDENT FROM THE FORMER NAVAL PERSON

1. Thank you for your telegram just received, I send you herewith Wavell's message to me of 29th. Please remember it was not written for your eye, but we have got to a point where none of that matters.

2. I entirely agree about the balance being maintained, especially as I guessed who [sic] you are leaving the supreme command vacancy for. Nothing must stand in the way of the big layout, namely, supreme commander, Wavell; deputy, unknown; naval, the Dutchman; Air, Brett, or whoever [sic] you choose. I have cabled Wavell on these lines, as it would be well to have his view before us before final decision.

3. I will reply to your paragraphs 3-7 inclusive after I have put them before the Cabinet on Monday. You may be sure there will be no disagreements between you and me.

4. Your paragraphs 8 and 9. Thank you so much for all your kindness. I cannot tell you how sorry I was to leave the White House. I enjoyed every minute of it, which is more than all of those whos [sic] portraits adorn the walls can say.[30]

President Roosevelt recommended Brett be placed in command of ABDACOM Air (ABDAIR), but General Brett demurred, preferring to remain Wavell's deputy. In this role he was responsible for administration, supply, and maintenance for air and ground forces.[31] It may indicate the difficult communications between the Pacific, Washington, DC, and London that Churchill's letter of 1 February 1942 does not recognize Brett's establishment as Wavell's deputy. Brett had originally sent a message to Arnold on 12 January 1942 reporting that he was serving as ABDACOM's deputy commander.[32] On the other hand, perhaps Churchill intended to outline what he hoped would be the somewhat permanent shape of the ABDACOM organization, independent of the individuals selected for the various positions within the command.

Despite Churchill's upbeat letter to Roosevelt, a week later Brereton had decided the Far East Air Force (FEAF) he commanded should be withdrawn from Java. Wavell and Brett both decried this recommendation as premature. Brereton's pessimism was borne out on 15 February 1942 when Singapore fell to the Japanese.[33] Brett sent his estimate of the situation to Marshall on 18 February 1942:

PALEMBANG AREA OF SOUTH SUMATRA WAS DEFENDED WITH ALL FORCES AVAILABLE AND THERE IS LITTLE LEFT TO PREVENT ITS

OCCUPATION DOWN TO SUNDA STRAIT [.] UNDOUBTEDLY EX-
TREMELY HEAVY LOSSES WERE INFLICTED ON THE ENEMY DUR-
ING THE ATTACK ON PALEMBANG WHICH MAY TEMPORARILY DE-
LAY FURTHER ADVANCE [.] THERE ARE NOW INDICATIONS OF
POSSIBLE JAPANESE ATTACK ON BALI [.] BALI IS POORLY DE-
FENDED BUT WITHIN STRIKING RANGE OF OUR AIR FORCES IN
EAST JAVA [.] SHOULD THIS ATTACK BE SUCCESSFUL IT WILL BE A
STEPPING STONE TO FURTHER ATTACK ON EAST JAVA [.] THERE-
FORE CONSIDERATION SHOULD BE GIVEN TO THE WORST POSSI-
BLE SITUATION WHICH IS AN ATTEMPTED INVASION ON JAVA BE-
FORE THE END OF THE MONTH [.][34]

The enemy occupied Bali, Borneo, and the Celebes by 19 February 1942 when the Japanese conducted a devastating air
raid on Darwin, Australia. Java had been cut off, and Wavell
dispatched a message to Churchill on 21 February 1942 that
"the defence of ABDACOM area has broken down and . . . the
defence of Java cannot now last long." He blamed the defeat on
the lack of air superiority and the failure of reinforcements.[35]

On 23 February 1942 General Brett left Java for Australia.
The final evacuation of Java by the AAF occurred 2 March 1942.
Although most of the supporting ground forces, including US
antiaircraft units, were left behind with elements of the Dutch
army to resist as long as possible, the Japanese soon impris-
oned them.[36] General Marshall authorized Brereton to go either
to India or Australia, and Brereton accepted Wavell's invitation
to come to India as AAF commander. Arnold preferred that
Brereton accompany Brett to Australia, but Brett and Brereton
had parted ways before either man received Arnold's instructions.[37]

Brett arrived in Melbourne on 24 February 1942, taking
command of US Army troops in Australia. Although ABDACOM
was dissolved on 25 February, Brett tried to assist the defenders on Java by diverting P-400s bound for India to Java. A convoy including 32 assembled P-40s on the deck of the aircraft
carrier *Langley* and 27 crated P-40s aboard the freighter *Sea
Witch* made for the island, but Japanese planes sank the *Langley* on 27 February, and the *Sea Witch* arrived 28 February only
to have her cargo destroyed by Allied forces fearing the crated
P-40s would fall into the hands of the approaching Japanese.[38]
Brett's combat frustrations in Java were presently followed by
more trials, but of a different sort. Brett was soon daunted by

the pivotal challenge of his career, fighting the war as MacArthur's Airman.

Notes

1. Rogers, *The Good Years*, 31–32. The strategic situation in the Philippines was somewhat confused because Congress had promised independence to that island nation after a 10-year probationary period. This prevented a military buildup in response to the Japanese aggression in Manchuria, but also made a withdrawal of US military presence unsatisfactory. The Philippine National Defense Act, passed during the first year of MacArthur's tour as military adviser, promoted the general to the rank of field marshal of the Philippine army. Even so, he was authorized a contingent of active duty US Army officers. This contingent included Maj Dwight D. Eisenhower, and eventually Lt Col Richard Sutherland. Ibid., 38–39.

2. Ibid., 44–45.

3. Green, "Prelude to Pearl Harbor Attack."

4. Ibid.

5. Ibid.

6. *Roanoke Times*, "General Brett is America's Top Soldier in Western Pacific."

7. Courtney, "Born to Fly," 39.

8. Green, "George Howard Brett, Lt. General, USA, AC, 1886–1963." According to notes in the Green Collection, Brett sent a message to Arnold from Cairo, Egypt, at 2100, 7 December 1941 stating that he planned to depart for Karachi, India, 8 December, return to Cairo 11 December, and proceed home to Washington, DC, 13 December unless otherwise instructed. It is not clear whether he knew of the Pearl Harbor attack when he submitted the message. Green, "Prelude to Pearl Harbor Attack."

9. Green, "Prelude to Pearl Harbor Attack."

10. Ibid.

11. Woollcombe, *The Campaigns of Wavell*, 162. Wavell was concerned the Chinese forces would be more trouble than they were worth, since they would not have any organic logistical support.

12. Craven and Cate, eds., *The Army Air Forces in World War II*, 227.

13. On 8 December 1941 Brereton's B-17s were mostly destroyed on the ground by a Japanese air attack. Brereton later blamed the misfortune on a delay by Sutherland and/or MacArthur, but in an 18 December 1941 letter to Arnold he makes no such allegation. He is quoted as writing, "General MacArthur has supported me in every possible way; I think we have his whole-hearted appreciation and support and I consider myself fortunate in having such an outstanding leader for my boss." Green, "Prelude to Pearl Harbor Attack."

14. Miller, "A 'Pretty Damn Able Commander' Lewis Hyde Brereton: Part II," 32–33. Ironically, the ARCADIA Conference, in Washington, DC, which sealed the agreement between Pres. Franklin Delano Roosevelt and British

prime minister Winston Churchill that Europe would take priority over the Pacific, was taking place at that moment. Craven and Cate, eds., *The Army Air Forces in World War II*, 227.

15. Courtney, "Born to Fly," 39.

16. Craven and Cate, eds., *The Army Air Forces in World War II*, 226.

17. Ibid., 367.

18. Green Collection. Roosevelt to Churchill, draft announcement, 23 January 1942, ARC Identifier 195022. The Green Collection indicates this memo was probably drafted by Eisenhower at the ARCADIA Conference. Green, "Prelude to Pearl Harbor Attack."

19. Shepard, "American, British, Dutch, and Australian Coalition," 6–7.

20. Miller, interview.

21. Shepard, "American, British, Dutch, and Australian Coalition," 6–7 and 39–43.

22. Message, ABDA-162, ABDACOM, 1 February 1942.

23. Green, "Prelude to Pearl Harbor Attack."

24. Shepard, "American, British, Dutch, and Australian Coalition," 43.

25. Green, "Prelude to Pearl Harbor Attack."

26. Miller, "A 'Pretty Damn Able Commander'," 34–35.

27. Green, "Prelude to Pearl Harbor Attack."

28. Craven and Cate, eds., *The Army Air Forces in World War II*, 367.

29. Woollcombe, *The Campaigns of Wavell*, 165–66.

30. Churchill to Roosevelt, *ABDACOM Command Arrangements*. Churchill's fascinating comment about "I guessed who you are leaving the supreme command vacancy for" seems contradictory on its face, since in his next phrase he designates Wavell as supreme commander. One might assume Roosevelt intends to designate MacArthur supreme commander after the presumptive failure of the Philippine defense. According to Woollcombe, Wavell was not favored by Churchill. The likewise expected failure of the ABDACOM mission would neatly result in Wavell's relief by MacArthur. Document is declassified.

31. Craven and Cate, eds., *The Army Air Forces in World War II*, 370–71. It seems very unusual that Brett would not accept the command Roosevelt recommended for him—perhaps Brett felt he would be more at home working the logistical issues that had dominated his career up to that time, or perhaps he regarded the ABDAIR command as less important than his position as ABDACOM deputy supreme commander.

32. Green, "Prelude to Pearl Harbor Attack."

33. Miller, "A 'Pretty Damn Able Commander'," 35.

34. Message, ABDA-432, ABDACOM 18 February 1942.

35. Miller, "A 'Pretty Damn Able Commander'," 35.

36. Craven and Cate, eds., *The Army Air Forces in World War II*, 370–71; Miller, telephone interview by author, 9 January 2004.

37. Miller, "A 'Pretty Damn Able Commander'," 35.

38. Green, "Prelude to Pearl Harbor Attack."

Chapter 5

Airpower and Antagonism in Australia

The war in the Pacific had thus far heavily favored the Japanese. General Brett had not given up, however, and set about establishing a command element in Melbourne. By 3 March 1942 he had formed an estimate of the situation and sent it to the War Department:

> Part 1. Immediate completion plans for defense of AUSTRALIA vital. Further support JAVA impossible. Estimate of risk of attack on northwest AUSTRALIA follows: Resistance in JAVA will probably cease within week. . . . Enemy air strength 500–600 planes. Allied 42 serviceable, mostly obsolete. Enemy ground forces 100,000, five divisions plus auxiliaries. Allied about 36,000 mostly native white troops, lack equipment. Enemy morale high, allied doubtful.
>
> ENEMY NAVAL FORCES: 3 to 5 aircraft carriers. 10 to 15 cruisers. 20 destroyers. Over 100 transports. . . . Enemy . . . can attack northwest AUSTRALIA within 3 weeks. First stage occupation WYNDHAM area for air bases and BROOME for flank protection, and occupation MILLINGIM GROOTE EYLANDT airdrome. Second stage, attack DARWIN.
>
> PART 5. Enemy bombed WYNDHAM and BROOME yesterday. American and allied planes damaged. Probable objective to harass evacuation from NETHERLANDS EAST INDIES and re-inforcements from AUSTRALIA. PORT MORESBY bombed yesterday. Conclude enemy will attack northwest AUSTRALIA soon.[1]

Brett's near-term prediction proved absolutely accurate. Japanese landings on Java beginning 1 March 1942 rapidly achieved success, and the Dutch army surrendered on 9 March 1942. His conclusion about the imminent invasion of Australia proved wrong, however. The Japanese had achieved their objective when they gained the oil and mineral wealth of the Netherlands East Indies, and their limited forces were already badly overextended.[2]

On the day before General Brett's departure from Java for Australia, General Marshall drafted orders for President Roosevelt's signature, ordering General MacArthur out of the Philippines to take command in Australia. On 24 February 1942 MacArthur requested a delay in complying with the order, and his staff began to make arrangements for the evacuation from Corregidor. The plan that was eventually executed entailed spiriting

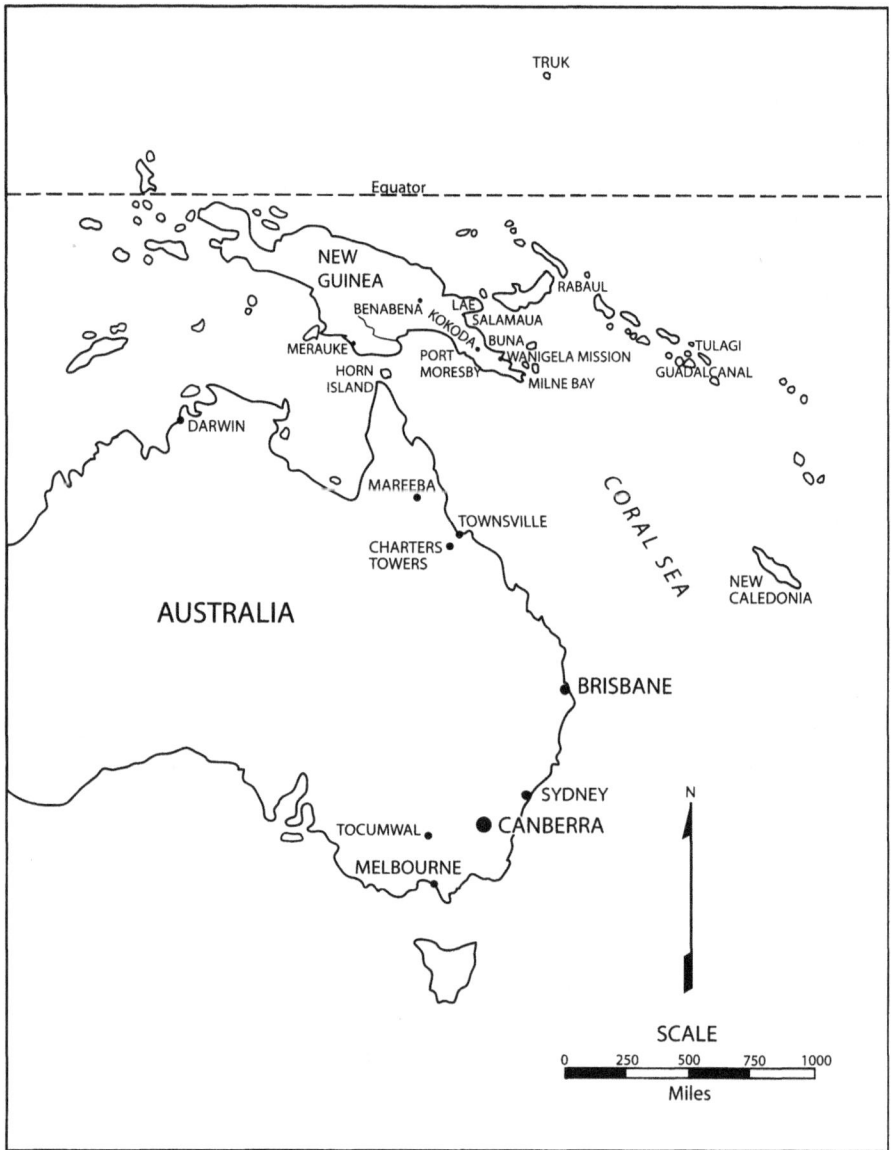

Figure 2. Australia and New Guinea map

MacArthur, his family, and key staff away from the fortress on patrol torpedo (PT) boats. They were delivered to the Del Monte airfield on Mindanao (still in American hands), where they transferred to aircraft to make the long flight to Australia. On 1

March 1942 chief of staff, United States Army Forces in the Far East (USAFFE), Gen Richard Sutherland, dictated the following message for General Brett to prepare for this contingency:

> You have probably surmised purpose of mission. Request detail best pilots and that best available planes be placed in top condition for trip. B-24's if available otherwise B-17's. Ferry mission only. Desire if possible initial landing on return to be south of combat zone. Anticipate call for arrival Mindanao about 15.[3]

General Brett had many other claims on his attention. At 0442 on 5 March 1942 the Japanese attacked Darwin, Australia. On the same date in the NEI 50 Japanese bombers and 12 fighters attacked friendly surface forces. General Brett reported 184 aircraft in commission for combat, of which 19 were B-17s and three were B-24s. He also sent a message labeled "IMPORTANT URGENT," requesting greater attention to the training of Australia-bound pilots because of the "alarming" number of pilot-induced aircraft accidents. Almost all of the pilots detailed to pursuit units had received no training in fighter aircraft.[4]

The fifth of March was a busy day for General Brett and was to turn more so with the additional requirement to respond to an inquiry from the War Department regarding the sinking of the *Langley*. His reply reads:

> FOR MARSHALL [.] LANGLEY proceeded after personal assurance Admiral Helfrich it would be suitably protected. 12 crew men, 30 pilots, 32 fighters aboard.
>
> Understand 27 crated P-40's unloaded by SEA WITCH at JAVA.
>
> Every effort being made to render assistance.
>
> Only one remaining Field JAVA.
>
> Bombing from northwest shoulder AUSTRALIA not considered possible, due to enemy action.[5]

Although the message that instigated this reply is not available, it seems obvious the War Department was urging Brett to continue and, if possible, improve his support for the beleaguered forces in the NEI. The last line of the message shows the Airman's inclination to husband his precious aircraft and crews. This inclination later brought him into direct conflict with General MacArthur and his brusque chief of staff, General Sutherland.

41

For the next 10 days Brett worked hard to formulate a strategy for the Southwest Pacific area, but he felt handicapped by a lack of experienced personnel. His close friend, Gen Ralph Royce, had his hands full with duties as Brett's chief of staff and "commander of air forces." On 7 March 1942 Brett urgently requested a general officer be flown from Washington, DC, to act as G-3. "He must be an Air Officer. Request serious consideration be given to Maj. Gen. Stratem[e]yer, Brig. Gen. Willis Hale, Brig. Gen. Edwards."[6] Meanwhile, Brett was also trying to nail down command arrangements for the Australia and New Zealand (ANZAC) area. In a message to the War Plans Division (WPD) he reported the prime minister of Australia wished to have a US Army officer placed in supreme command of the area, and sought the concurrence of Roosevelt and Churchill in the matter.[7]

Simultaneously, General Brett was fighting a turf battle with the US Navy. Among the flurry of situation reports, personnel reports, and one message reporting that censorship had been imposed, Brett requested he be issued confirmation that the B-17s that recently arrived from Hawaii had been placed under his command: "This confirms that 12 B-17's recently sent from HAWAII to Australia are to operate in Australia [quotes radiogram from Australian Legation, Washington to Chief Naval Staff, MELBOURNE] and requests that these bombers and crews be placed under Brett's command."[8] This struggle aggravated Brett's inability to supply the MacArthur evacuation mission with the "best planes" that had been demanded by Sutherland. In his *True Magazine* article "The MacArthur I Knew," Brett tells the story of his clash with the Navy:

> From the wreckage of Java I had brought a dozen B-17s. . . .They were in pretty bad shape. MacArthur would not be pleased with the best we could send. . . . He hated to fly, suffered from airsickness, and would not get into a plane unless he knew it was perfect. He had his wife and child with him, and the trip would be dangerous every minute. He would want bright new ships, fresh off the assembly line. . . .

> I looked over my B-17s. I didn't have any B-24s. There wasn't a bomber in the lot fit for the Philippines trip. . . .

> There was just one way out. Twelve new Flying Fortresses had just arrived in Australia, but they were assigned to the Navy. To a civilian this might not seem to be much of a problem. . . . In fact it was. At that time the United States Fleet was in the Coral Sea, trying to make contact with the Japs.

> I went to Admiral Herbert Fairfax Leary, and told him I had to get Mac-Arthur out of the Philippines, and chances were a thousand to one he would not fly in any of the bombers I had. Could I borrow three to bring him to Australia?
>
> Leary had the reputation of saying no to all requests, unless he could see that the Navy would benefit by his acquiescence.
>
> "I'd like to help you, Brett," he said, "but it is quite impossible. . . . You'll have to do the best you can with what you have."[9]

Brett's unsuccessful negotiation with Leary was interspersed with serious concerns about the overall US logistics strategy. On 11 March 1942 Brett sent a message to the WPD expressing his belief that American efforts should be focused on Australia, while British-made equipment should be supplied exclusively to India. On the same day, he reported a successful raid led by Maj Richard Chamberlain that pitted eight B-17s against Salamaua Harbor, New Guinea, resulting in destruction and damage to Japanese shipping with no losses to the US forces. He also desperately requested that 10,000 gallons of Prestone coolant be shipped to Australia as soon as possible.[10]

About the same time, MacArthur, his family, and key members of his staff were escaping from Corregidor aboard a small flotilla of US Navy vessels. They arrived at Del Monte, Mindanao, sometime on 12 March 1942, where they discovered the flight of bombers ordered for their trip to Australia consisted of only one malfunctioning B-17. Although four aircraft had been dispatched for the mission, two experienced mechanical failures, and one, commanded by Lt Henry Godman, ran out of fuel and ditched near Mindanao, killing two members of the crew.[11] Brett recounts the message he received from MacArthur, "Only one of four planes arrived, and that with an inexperienced pilot comma no brakes and supercharger not repeat not functioning stop This plane was returned to you by Gen. Sharpe, since it was not repeat not suitable for the purpose intended stop. . . . This trip is most important and desperate and must be set up with the greatest of care lest it end in disaster."[12]

Brett took the message as a rebuke, and Sutherland's stenographer, Master Sergeant Paul Rogers, asserts that it was intended as such. In his message to Marshall explaining the problem, however, MacArthur made an excuse for Brett:

I am informing Brett but request you inform him of group to be transported and order him to dispatch suitable planes if on hand, otherwise that you make such planes available to him. . . . The best three planes in the United States or Hawaii should be made available with completely adequate and experienced crews. . . . My presence in Del Monte should be kept completely secret and every means taken to create belief that I am still in Luzon. Pursuant to your order I did not inform Brett of mission and it would appear that he was ignorant of importance.[13]

According to Brett's own account, he was well aware of the character and sensitivity of the mission. After MacArthur made contact with Marshall, Brett found Leary much more forthcoming. "Back I went to Adm. Leary. I expected the same answer I'd had before, but was prepared to get tougher. But Leary didn't give me a single 'no.' Perhaps he had heard directly from Washington."[14]

Ultimately MacArthur and his party were safely transported to Australia, arriving 17 March 1942 at Batchelor Field near Darwin in two B-17s. After a short rest, they flew on to Alice Springs, where the group switched to rail transportation and proceeded to Melbourne.[15] MacArthur's deputy chief of staff, Brig Gen Richard J. Marshall, had flown ahead from Alice Springs to Melbourne. He rejoined MacArthur's train in Adelaide to give MacArthur a briefing. Receiving the news that only 25,000 American troops and fewer than 250 combat aircraft were in Australia, along with the distressing fact that all but one division of Australia's regular forces were engaged in the Middle East, MacArthur reportedly responded, "God have mercy on us!"[16]

On the day MacArthur landed at Batchelor Field, Brett presented a message to Australian Prime Minister John Curtin informing him of MacArthur's arrival and requesting on President Roosevelt's behalf that Curtin nominate MacArthur to supreme command of all Allied forces in the Southwest Pacific, if such was in accord with the wishes of the Australian people.[17] If Brett expected a cordial greeting from the new supreme commander, he was soon disabused of the notion. MacArthur arrived in Melbourne on 21 March 1942 to much fanfare and excitement. After making a short speech to the press and greeting Australian officials, MacArthur and his family headed to their new quarters for a rest. Brett was taken aback when he offered to accompany MacArthur and Sutherland in their limousine and was curtly refused. Brett wrote, "That was a dash of cold water. After all, I was the senior officer from whom MacArthur was taking over command. . . . Later in the day Brig. Gen. Ralph Royce and I went to pay our respects to the new supreme commander. We waited rather uncomfortably for quite a while, but, when it became apparent that MacArthur did not intend to see us, we left our cards, and departed. I'll admit that I was irked and disappointed."[18]

MacArthur's frustration was not exclusively in Brett's imagination. At 0243 on 21 March, apparently before his arrival in Melbourne, the new commander filed a report to General Marshall describing the arrangements he had made in the Philippines and indicating his exasperation with the organization he had found in Australia:

> In Australia I have found the Air Corps in a most disorganized condition and it is most essential as a fundamental and primary step that General Brett be relieved of his other duties in order properly to command and direct our air effort. His headquarters in Melbourne is too far from the scene of air activity to perform most effectively the functions of organization, training and combat. I propose to relieve him immediately of all duties pertaining to ground forces and to have him establish his headquarters in the forward area in some locality he may select. I propose to assign Gen. Barnes to command U.S. Army Ground Forces. . . .

> Request immediate approval of this organization as a fundamental step in order to bring some order into what is at present a most uncoordinated and ineffective system which is a menace to the safety of this country. I will later and in more detail inform you of glaring deficiencies and make recommendations for their rectification. . . .[19]

Brett accepted MacArthur's displeasure philosophically. There was, after all, a great deal of work to do. On 22 March 1942 two B-17s attacked Rabaul, providing some good tactical intelligence but failing to report any destruction. The next day a raid on the Lae aerodrome, New Guinea, reportedly destroyed nine enemy aircraft on the ground. This encouraging news was dwarfed by the continuing disaster in the NEI. Brett reported the Japanese invaders had captured an oil refinery and its large stock virtually intact.[20] During that week Brett had been working hard to inform Washington, DC, of his great need for transport aircraft, since the Australian infrastructure and the threat from the Japanese made airlift the most convenient means of transporting supplies. Acquiring some cargo aircraft from the Dutch airline that had been operating in NEI, Brett requested permission to activate a transport squadron with personnel and equipment on hand. He also asked Washington, DC, to furnish personnel and equipment for a second transport squadron.[21]

Soon MacArthur requested a meeting with his air commander. Brett recollects that it took the new supreme commander eight days from his arrival to send for him, but he dates the meeting as 25 March 1942—four days after MacArthur's arrival in Melbourne. MacArthur was agitated and castigated Brett for disloyalty. MacArthur ostensibly believed Brett was envious because he had not been designated supreme commander. Brett replied angrily that he had turned down Prime Minister Curtin's offer of the post and could produce the message traffic to prove it. MacArthur went on to complain about the state of the air force:

> "They lack discipline, organization, purposeful intent," he said. I [Brett] thought of what my boys in Java had done. A few combat-weary men, flying worn-out planes, on which they had to work all night to even get into the air. Youngsters in ships that were outclassed in maneuverability by the Zeros. . . . Yet, for every plane and pilot they lost, my boys destroyed six times as many Japs.
>
> Discipline, organization, purposeful intent! No men ever had more.
>
> "There was never a time in the Philippines," MacArthur went on, "when I gave the air force a mission that was carried out successfully. I could never persuade Brereton to disperse his aircraft properly, and he was always negligent in the protection of airfields and equipment."
>
> This, flatly, I did not believe. I had known Louis [sic] Hyde Brereton for years. . . . Brereton's version of what had happened in the Philippines was entirely different than MacArthur's. . . .
>
> Then, the General turned the guns of his wrath on Adm. Hart. . . . It didn't take a psychoanalyst to figure out the trend of MacAthur's thoughts. Through no fault of his, the Philippines campaign had been lost. Defeat raked his spirit raw. Besides, he was abnormally sensitive to criticism. Blaming others is a defense mechanism.[22]

Despite the rocky interview recounted by Brett, his audience with MacArthur ended on a positive note, with Brett volunteering to go to Townsville, Australia "at once," and the Airman left convinced his wide-ranging efforts would be appreciated by the supreme commander.[23]

Social policy, as well as air operations and logistics, fell under Brett's broad purview as USAFIA commander. Australians, unused to the American attitudes toward African-Americans, were starting to react negatively to the strained relationship between

African-American and white American troops. Brett's recommendation was to remove all African-American troops from Australia for duty in India or New Caledonia. The same day Brett sent an urgent request for new reconnaissance aircraft, to include long-range fuel tanks. Two days later Brett's lone B-24 was lost at sea near Broome, Australia, apparently as a result of enemy action. Only one survivor was reported, 16 Airmen were presumed dead. As the month of March came to a close, Brett received yet more bad news. A shipment of B-17s from Hawaii to Australia had been halted, pending replacements arriving in Hawaii. A War Department note in the margin states "3/[2]8/42. Reply: Suspending dispatch of heavy bomber pending reconsiderations of allocation. Will be advised as to revised allocations and schedules of delivery."[24] By 29 March 1942 Brett's staff had consolidated its review of lessons learned up to that point in the Pacific. Brig Gen Harold H. George and Brig Gen Eugene Eubank submitted a list which quickly garnered the interest of General Arnold. In the margin of the message summary the AAF's commanding general scrawled: "I want to see the original of this message – HHA." Most of the lessons related to deficient training and equipment.[25]

Then-Col Frederick H. Smith Jr. gave some insight into Brett's headquarters and his operating style during March 1942. He reported to Brett as commander of the newly arrived Eighth Pursuit Group, intending to describe the severe equipment and personnel deficiencies he was facing. Instead, he received a lecture on safety from the Air Corps general, and a shocking insight into the state of the command:

> I got down to Melbourne and went immediately to General Brett's headquarters, and he received me right away. I started to tell him about my heavy equipment missing, and this that and the other, when he said, "Now, I am going to talk first, see." He said, "There will be no training accidents, and I mean none, ZERO." I said, "General Brett, I can't make a commitment like that. I have got 80 pilots I don't even know. I'm just picking them up and I have got to train them; and there will be an accident or two. I assure you I will do my damdest [sic]." He said, "If there are accidents you won't be a Group Commander." I said, "Very well, sir." I turned on my heel and went out of his office and passed his deputy's office, Ralph Royce.
>
> But what did he do but give me the identical, same speech? I went on down to the Chief of Staff. . . . Well anyway, he says, "Oh Freddie, I am awful sorry I have to go to an important Allied Conference meeting." But

he says, "I have got experts right outside here who will handle any of the questions that you have about personnel, intelligence, materiel, anything." I said, "O.K." So I went out to this outer office and here were four first lieutenants. Each of them had a little desk in front of them: one said "A-1," one said "A-2," one said "A-3," and one said "A-4." I went to the personnel man and I said, "When do I get my 80 crew chiefs, 80 armorers, and 80 pilots?" He said he did not know but he would check on it. I didn't ask the intelligence officer anything, there wasn't any point in that. I asked the operations officer what other airdromes I would have access to in the vicinity of Brisbane. He didn't know, but he would look it up for me. I asked the materiel A-4 what he was doing about getting my heavy equipment to me. He said, "Well, where is it, Colonel Smith?" I said, "Well, I happen to have found out from Colonel Sneed that it is in Perth, Australia, which is four states away from us, four different gauges, and I suggest you get on your horse and get going to get that stuff all shipped to me in Brisbane." Well, I was pretty dammed [sic] heartsick.[26]

In the first weeks of April, Brett participated in a four-day conference to sort out the command arrangements for the Southwest Pacific area (SWPA), which focused mainly on the duties and responsibilities of the supreme commander, SWPA.[27] At the same time, MacArthur was starting to exert his influence on the tone of message traffic coming from Australia. In his first message with the point of origin labeled "Australia," MacArthur makes it clear there is a new power at the helm, "Reorganization and regroupment Australian forces under way. I have suggested they be brought to full strength, that intensive officer training program be initiated and incompetents be eliminated. General public attitude of defeatism being replaced by growing optimism and self reliance."[28] While the "replacement" of defeatism with "optimism" may seem like a bombastic claim, the morale of the Australian people was buoyed by MacArthur's arrival; Australia also received a substantial increase in reinforcements from that time forward.[29]

Brett had hoped MacArthur would be impressed with his hard work so far, and with what AAF and Royal Australian Air Force (RAAF) personnel were doing with very limited resources. It was not to be. By 10 April 1942 MacArthur had already inspected some of Brett's establishment, and he was dismayed to find a dearth of American officers in command. Brett expressed his concern that this problem would hold up MacArthur's plan to move north aggressively to confront the Japanese: ". . . there is not a single station or area commanded by an AMERICAN officer. Although moving fighting squadrons into north-eastern and north-western AUSTRALIA impossible through lack of qualified officers to assume command stations which are mainly occupied by American units." In the same message, which MacArthur signed for transmission, Brett insisted this circumstance was lowering American morale, and requested Arnold reply to MacArthur with a solution.[30]

Despite Brett's personnel and supply problems MacArthur was determined to continue support of the forlorn contingent still struggling in the Philippines. On 29 March 1942 General Sutherland shocked Brett by ordering him to send a bombing mission against the Philippines immediately. Brett refused, but Sutherland shot back, "General MacArthur promised the Filipino people he would be back. If we send a bombing mission it will prove they have not been forgotten." Brett drug his feet as long as he could, but finally late in April 10 B-25s and two B-17s conducted a raid against Cebu and Davao City in the Philippines. Gen Ralph Royce, Brett's chief of staff, personally led the mission because Brett and Royce both considered it so dangerous.[31]

Brett estimated the bombers had been less than 30 percent effective in all of their attacks, and complained that the ordnance was inadequate. He asked for "development of armour piercing type bomb" and noted Japanese air strength was unresponsive: "No air opposition until second day of operations in area." He ended his report with the refrain his audience in Washington, DC, was probably becoming numb to: "This mission was hastily organized—pilots and bombers were new to the aircraft and to each other[—]it is believed that crews trained on the aircraft and as teams would have obtained better results."[32]

The raid came too late for the warriors on Bataan, who surrendered to the Japanese on 8 April 1942.[33] While Brett was organizing the heroic but ultimately ineffective raid on the Philippines, MacArthur was urging Washington, DC, to help him mount a major offensive to retake the Philippines before the garrison on Corregidor was defeated. On 13 April he wrote: "Under these circumstances I regard it as useless to attempt further general supply by blockade running although an attempt will be made to provide additional antiaircraft ammunition. I believe the only alternatives which present themselves are a major effort involving grand strategic considerations to be executed within the next two months, or the acceptance of ultimate defeat in MANILA BAY."[34]

There was to be no change in the grand strategic plan, however, and Brett continued to struggle through personnel problems, cabling on 18 April 1942 that officers intended to stand up two new pursuit squadrons had been farmed out to units already in Australia. He recommended the forthcoming pursuit units be reorganized stateside. On 20 April 1942 he sent an encouraging message to Arnold, reporting that Royce had found the B-25 to be a superb performer during the Philippine raid.[35] Arnold was soon to receive a much less encouraging message from Brett's superior, however:

> Air Force personnel in this area is in a state of indifferent training and very loose organization. Several months needed to produce operational efficiency that is satisfactory. In order to execute its missions with precision and accuracy and secure value from airplanes at its disposal, it is fundamental that this force should be placed in a state of sufficiently advanced training.

In the margin someone, probably General Arnold, noted "Kuter to analyze, action copy to A-1."[36] On 26 April another message followed, explaining that MacArthur was taking control of pilot assignments: "Will use all available pilots in this area to best possible advantage by shifting among various units. Australian programme [sic] of Organization and review of pilots available makes any surplus of Australian pilots unlikely."[37]

On 30 April, Brett requested all correspondence pertaining to "Air Force technical questions, supply and organization be addressed Commander Allied Air Forces, Melbourne. A new organization Allied Air Force, Melbourne was established."[38] Over a month after his interview with MacArthur, Brett was establishing a new organization in Melbourne, despite the fact he had promised the commander he would lead the air force from Townsville. On the same day, Brett sent a cable complaining that a unit had arrived missing 108 people, even though it had departed Selfridge, Michigan, at full strength. He noted this was not the first time this had happened with Air Corps units.[39]

On 1 May 1942, MacArthur sent a report to Marshall regarding the forces under his command. Although he found fault with his small naval forces, and dismissed the Australian air force as limited to coastal defense, he reported the few ground troops at his disposal were in satisfactory condition. The US air force component, however, received his specific attention: "US Air Forces consist of 2 (*Heavy*) bombardment groups, 2 (*Medium*) bomb groups (less 2 sqdns) and 3 pursuit groups with 100% T/O (*Table of Allowance*) operating aircraft plus 50% in reserve, there having been no specific number assigned as wastage. Training and organization below standard and will require about 4 months intensive effort to reach satisfactory condition."[40]

May was an eventful month in the Pacific war, and the Navy successfully engaged the Japanese in the Battle of the Coral Sea south of the Solomon Islands, 7–8 May 1942.[41] Perhaps in consequence of this positive development, and perhaps because of concerns about Brett's performance, Marshall sent a message to MacArthur requesting a daily update informing the US Joint Chiefs of Staff of any land, air, and naval operations as well as enemy movements. Specifically for Brett he added the following: "For purposes of future planning and building up of necessary experience tables it is important that all operations by United States Air Forces be reported daily to include types and numbers engaged, nature of target, kind and amount of resistance, and our own and enemy losses."[42]

In May Brett submitted a detailed report of the situation in the theater, including lessons learned in the war up to that point. The report also described the layout of air force units and the state of training. The personnel situation drove Brett to a fateful decision that later subjected him to censure from his fellow Airmen. Lacking capable copilots, Brett decided to combine Australian flyers with American crews. "The necessity has now arisen for considering the use of RAAF co-pilots where possible. Organization of intermediate headquarters in conjunction with the RAAF will place an additional strain on the supply of officer personnel, and, lacking both administrative personnel and technicians, means the use of pilot personnel."[43] Predictably, the idea of pulling pilots off the line for staff duty was unpopular with some of the pilots involved. Colonel Smith described his shock at being pulled back from fighter command at Port Moresby, New Guinea. He was designated the senior air staff officer of the RAAF units in the Sydney area, but when he arrived he discovered the post was already filled by an Australian. Despite his complaints, he was unable to get out of the job. Royce told him, "No, Freddie, General Brett has made up his mind. He is going to mix up all these people, Aussies as well as Americans, and that is where you are going to be."[44]

Late in May Brett reported on a number of issues, including B-26 fuel tank problems, B-26 torpedo testing, and continuing personnel shortages.[45] At the end of the month Brett sent a message to Arnold from MacArthur's headquarters reporting problems with AAF senior leadership:

> This is a reply to urad 1712 of the 11th (re inadequacies of general officers and the death of Gen. George.)
>
> Recommend for assignment here Col. Ennis Whitehead in the grade of brigadier general as the replacement for Gen. George.
>
> Major General Stratemeyer is especially desired. Conditions and vacancy warrant his assignment.
>
> For approximately five weeks Gen. [Rush B.] Lincoln has been confined to the hospital, and complete recovery is questionable due to his age. A report will follow at later date re his possible return to the U.S. without prejudice.
>
> Since there has been insufficient time for accurate appraisal of the work of [Brigadier General Michael] Scanlon, report will be made later in his case.
>
> Hoyt and Eubank not deemed suitable for promotion. Their return to the U.S. is recommended and replacements are required.
>
> Many difficulties have arisen in operation and administration, both in Air Corps and RAAF, due to youth and inexperience of group and squadron commanders. This has caused a loss of operational efficiency. It is thought that this situation can be corrected by a suitable inspection section for Allied Air Force Hq.[46]

Brett's troubles became worse on 1 June 1942 when he received an official reprimand from MacArthur:

> PERSONAL AND CONFIDENTIAL:
>
> Dear Brett:
>
> Your attention is invited to the fact that in giving the interview ascribed to you in the enclosed newspaper clipping without first submitting it to this headquarters you violated the explicit instructions contained in standing orders. Such indifference in execution of directives by senior commanders tends to demoralize the discipline of the entire force. The statement of relative losses and prediction of future results by an officer of your rank and position gives valuable guidance to the enemy.
>
> Sincerely,
>
> DOUGLAS MacARTHUR.[47]

The article containing Brett's interview is not to be found with the reprimand. Whether the reprimand was drafted by MacArthur or not is unknown, although the tone of the prose indicates it was.

Nevertheless, Brett was soon to receive a flurry of correspondence from Sutherland hinting at his incompetence, or accusing him outright of failure to comply with orders. On 3 June 1942 Sutherland requested Brett personally explain why P-39s and P-400s were not dependable for escort duties over Lae and Salamaua since they could be equipped with belly tanks to increase their range. On the same day, Sutherland sent a tabulation of B-17E service rates which he noted were exceptionally low, indicating "something basically at fault with the equipment, maintenance or operation of this type of airplane." Again, he stated Brett should provide an explanation in person. To add insult to injury, Col Burdette M. Fitch, MacArthur's adjutant general, sent a message to Brett condescendingly explaining the purpose of decorations, and demanding elements of Brett's command submit award nominations immediately after combat missions.[48]

On 4 June 1942 Sutherland sent Brett a recitation of B-17 operations from the previous week, complaining that "according to operations reports, no attack has been made upon the airdromes at Rabaul in compliance with Operations Instructions No. 8. It is desired that action be taken without delay to execute that order." On the next day, Sutherland issued a stilted response to Brett's demand that SWPA headquarters "secure a suitable fighter aircraft" to meet recurring Japanese attacks at Port Moresby. Sutherland quoted Brett's own message traffic claiming hits on Japanese aircraft, and reminded Brett of a recently transmitted report on the "operational and technical design of fighter planes" forwarded to Washington, DC, on Brett's behalf. The SWPA chief of staff promised headquarters support, but insisted: "Further action looking to the technical design and development of aircraft will have to be initiated by you."[49]

As might be expected, Brett promptly responded with a two-page explanation of why P-39s and P-40s were inadequate for escort duty over Lae and Salamaua even with belly tanks. An elementary lesson in fighter operations, the letter underscored the ignorance of air operations betrayed by Sutherland's missive. Combat fuel consumption, evasive action, weather diversions, as well as the need to jettison tanks during combat engagements, were all cited as factors limiting aircraft range. Pointedly, Brett's response was delivered by mail, and signed by his new chief of staff, Air Vice Marshal W. Bostock, RAAF. In another letter, Bostock answered Sutherland's complaint about the lack of attacks against Rabaul indicating crew fatigue and excessive B-26 fuel consumption brought on by worn engines had prevented the attack thus far. Bostock promised "daylight attacks of aerodromes and installations in the Rabaul area within the next three or four days."[50]

Possibly stung by the reprimand he had received, Brett complained to MacArthur on 9 June 1942 that the Australian Air Minister, Mr. Arthur S. Drakeford, had published statements congratulating RAAF and Dutch aircrews, but making no mention of American efforts. Brett requested MacArthur's action to prevent damage to US morale. MacArthur responded with a gracious note, declaring himself "in complete accord with the views contained in your note" and adding "you can completely rely upon me to see that our own national forces will receive full credit for everything they accomplish."[51] Despite MacArthur's cordiality, the war of words between Sutherland and Brett had escalated into a formal directive, signed simply "General, U.S. Army, Commander-in-Chief." The directive recounted the sorties between 4 and 8 June, observing that all were reconnaissance instead of attack. Although Lae was attacked by two B-17s on 9 June, the Vunakanau Airdrome, Rabaul was still untouched. Intelligence indicated "a very large number of aircraft" present there. The closing line states: "You are directed to attack that target with all available planes without further delay."[52]

In response, Brett wrote and signed a memorandum recounting the actions his command had taken up to that time in efforts to comply with Instruction No. 8 General Headquarters Operation, issued 29 May 1942. He gives the details in six chronological points, following up with five separate mitigating points. On the fifth page of the response, Brett recommends a new bombing policy which would allow daylight attacks against Rabaul only by formations of six or more B-17s. In his final paragraph, on page six, Brett requests quick approval of his recommendation or the issuance of a new directive.[53] Even as

Brett tried to assuage the irritation of General Headquarters about the lack of action against Rabaul, fresh troubles were brewing. On 13 June 1942 Colonel Fitch sent an order to Brett demanding an aircraft for headquarters' use: "Your attention is invited to a letter from this headquarters, subject as above, dated 17 May 1942 in which you were directed to provide an airplane for use by this headquarters and to report the date upon which the plane would become available. You are directed to comply with that order without further delay."[54]

In response, Bostock offered either a B-17C, number 40-2072, that had recently been reengined and would be available by 15 June 1942, or a passenger DC-3 with new engines, radio, and heater. Bostock opines, "This machine has a 1000 mile safe range, and it is believed to be more suitable for the purpose specified than the B-17C." Fitch responded two days later that the B-17 had been inspected and was found to be unsatisfactory, and that the DC-3 would be inspected on 18 June. The officer who performed the inspection on the rejected B-17C was Henry Godman, the pilot that had been rescued from the waves during the first attempt to pick up MacArthur at Del Monte on Mindanao. His memorandum states: "I personally counted over 400 holes in the ship." He continues, "The ship is considered a 'lemon' by all pilots."[55]

Finally Brett received what seemed like some positive feedback from Sutherland. Brett's letter of 24 May 1942 had prompted a conference between MacArthur and Sutherland, and MacArthur had agreed with Brett's recommendations concerning daylight bombing on Rabaul, and further agreed to issue "a new directive covering reconnaissance missions." Sutherland's letter concludes with the statement that the current directive will stand until enemy dispositions make it necessary to issue a new one. Confusingly, Sutherland refers to the directive as "Operations Instructions No. 6" instead of "Operations Instructions No. 8" throughout the communication to Brett.[56]

Any comfort General Brett might have taken in winning MacArthur's approval was illusory, however. Two days before MacArthur had sent a long message to Washington, DC, complaining about recent promotions of Airmen to the rank of brigadier general. Almost certainly drafted by MacArthur himself, the message refers to communications between Arnold and Brett contemplating "a change in existing promotion policies in this area as they affect Air Corps personnel" as "dangerous to apply in a combat area under battle service conditions." MacArthur concludes the two-page jeremiad with this statement: ". . . I invite attention to the fact that the recent appointments of four general officers of the Air Corps of this command were made without any previous knowledge on my part and in my own opinion, and I think in that of the majority of the rank and file, do not represent a fair evaluation of either the service or the capacity of some of the officers involved. Such incidents tend not only to disrupt the composure of the command but to jeopardize its unity of purpose. MacArthur."[57]

If Brett was aware of MacArthur's displeasure it did not prevent him from working on the continuing logistical and personnel problems he faced. On 19 June 1942 Brett sent word to Washington, DC, that replacements must be expedited; he requested specific information about replacement flow and the level of training for aircrews to slated for duty in SWPA. Two days later, Brett responded to Arnold's query about whether torpedoes were being used in operations by explaining that training was still underway. On 25 June 1942 Brett sent messages explaining B-26 deficiencies, fuel line clamp problems on B-17Es, and requesting a follow-up on an April message requesting civilian engine overhaul personnel be sent to Australia. The reminder got Arnold's attention, and he scrawled "Snyder see me, HHA" in the margin.[58]

Whether or not Brett suspected MacArthur wanted to replace him with a new air commander, the War Department got the message. On 26 June 1942 MacArthur sent a long message addressed to "Plans." Beginning with a diatribe about the lack of aircraft and replacements, he goes on to say that good reconnaissance work has been conducted with very limited assets by the Navy and the RAAF. Combat air forces, however, have been used with extreme conservatism because of maintenance difficulties:

> The efficiency of Air Corps in this area is only average. The Air Corps commander contributes [sic] this to failure to supply him with properly trained personnel or adequate equipment and supplies. This has been reflected constantly in reports made by Gen. Brett to Gen. Arnold and by occasional radios by myself. The deficiencies, if existent, do not appertain either to tactical or strategical handling of Air Corps components

56

but to inherent weakness in the Air Corps itself, which matters are largely beyond the control of this headquarters.[59]

Whether MacArthur's use of the word "contributes" instead of "attributes" was deliberate, or whether it arose merely from a copyist's error, Marshall took the supreme commander's meaning. On 29 June 1942 Marshall radioed back to MacArthur:

> THIS COMMUNICATION TO BE READ BY GENERAL MACARTWUR [sic] AND CODE CLERK ONLY PERIOD DESIRE YOUR VIEWS AND RECOMMENDATIONS ON POSSIBLE REPLACEMENT OF BRETT BY GENERAL FRANK ANDREWS PERIOD REPLY TO ME PERSONALLY MARSHALL[60]

Marshall had been reluctant to replace his friend and fellow VMI alumni, but throughout the late winter and spring pressure had been coming from Secretary of War Henry L. Stimson to recall Brett. At the beginning of February 1942 Stimson confided to his diary:

> After the war council meeting I had a talk with Patterson, McCloy and Lovett about Brett, in whom I have never had much confidence. It is a delicate question because Marshall likes him and backs him up, but I found that no one of the three above mentioned, thought that he was very good for much. After that I called in Arnold, and on the same subject, he gave a b[e]tter estimate of Brett as a commander, although he admitted he was no good in executive work. He has apparently made good as a squadron and group commander, but failed at Panama and as head of the Air Corps. . . . I told Marshall as gently as I could my fears about Brett, and the confirmatory statements that I had received from Patterson, McCloy and Lovett. . . . He, of course, defended Brett, but with perfect poise and equanimity. . . .[61]

There was doubt about Brett's viability in command even within the ranks of his subordinates. When Brig Gen Ross G. Hoyt returned to the United States on 6 June 1942 he reported on the state of affairs in the Pacific. Arnold asked him point-blank if Brett should be relieved. Hoyt told Arnold that either Brett or MacArthur must go.[62] MacArthur replied immediately in the affirmative to Marshall's query, following his response with an evaluation of Brett. It bears repeating in its entirety:

> FOR GENERAL MARSHALL ONLY STOP I WOULD PREFER ANDREWS TO BRETT AND BELIEVE A CHANGE HERE WOULD STRENGTHEN THE AIR COMPONENT REPLYING YOUR THREE ZERO THREE TWENTYNINTH STOP I KNOW BOTH MEN INTIMATELY AND I HAVE NO DOUBT WHATEVER THAT ANDREWS CMA WHILE NOT NATURALLY AS BRILLIANTLY GIFTED AS BRE[TT] CMA POSSESSES THOSE ELEMENTS OF BASIC CHARACTER WHICH CONSTITUTE A BETTER FIGHTING COMMANDER UNDER BATTLE CONDITIONS STOP BRETT

IS UNQUESTIONABLY HI[GHLY] QUALIFIED AS AN AIR TECHNICIAN AND IN AIR ADMINISTRATIVE DUTIES OF A PRODU[C]TIVE OR SUP-PLY CHARACTER SEMICOLON HE IS AN UNUSUALLY HARD WORKER BUT HIS VERY INDUSTRY LEADS HIM TO CONCENTRATE AT TIMES UPON UNIMPORTANT DETAILS WHICH TEND TO OBSCURE A TRUE PERSPECTIVE OF MORE IMPORTANT MATTERS SEMICOLON HE IS NATURALLY INCLINED TOWARD MORE OR LESS HARMLESS IN-TRIGUE AND HAS A B[ENT] CMA DUE PERHAPS TO HIS DELIGHTFUL PERSONALITY CMA FOR SOCIAL ENTERTAINMENT AND THE EASY WAY OF LIFE SEMICOLON HE IS UNPOPULAR WITH THE AUSTRALIAN ADM[I]NISTRATION WHO RESENT HIS LACK OF FORTHRIGHTNESS AND HE DOES NOT COMMAND T[HE] CONFIDENCE OF THE YOUNGER AND FIGHTING ELEMENTS OF THE AIR CORPS HERE STOP WOULD RATE HIS SERVICE DURING THE LAST THREE MONTHS UNDER MY COMMAND AS ON[LY] AVERAGE STOP HIS RELATIONSHIP WITH THE NAVY COMPONENT IS POOR STOP HIS RELATIONS WITH MY OWN HEADQUARTERS HAVE BEEN PERSONALLY MOST CORDIAL BUT PROFESSIONALLY HE HAS BEEN EVASIVE STOP ALTHOUGH BRETT HAS A VERY LARGE STAFF I DO NOT CONSIDER IT PARTICULARLY COMPETENT STOP THIS MAY BE DUE TO HIS INABILITY TO SELECT AND PLACE THE RIGHT MEN IN KEY POSITIONS OR POSSI[BLY] HE IS UNABLE PROPERLY TO COORDINATE THEM STOP ANDREWS IS A TYPE OF COMMAN[DER] WHO NEEDS A COMPETENT CHIEF OF STAFF AND OPERATIONS OFFICER STOP IN CASE [THIS] CHANGE IS MADE I SUGGEST THAT HE BE PERMITTED TO BRING THESE TWO STAFF OFFICERS WITH HIM AND THAT MEN OF CORRESPONDING RANK HERE BE RETURNED WITH BRETT MACARTHUR[63]

The evaluation's litany of Brett's shortcomings is covered with the gauze of left-handed compliments. The obvious con-flict between Sutherland and Brett is ignored in the fiction that claimed Brett's relations with MacArthur's headquarters had been "most cordial." When MacArthur accused Brett of intrigue, and followed up with a discussion of the Australian administra-tion's resentment of the Airman it is possible MacArthur was referring to the labor government of Australian Prime Minister John Curtin. Gen George C. Kenney told historian D. Clayton James that Brett had become friends with members of the Aus-tralian conservative party. According to Kenney:

> I think he [Brett] made his initial mistake in sort of spurning this Labor government crowd and taking up with the Conservative crowd, who had been ousted by the Labor Party and who were not going to get back into power. But Brett figured they were, so he accepted entertainment from them and entertained them in return and became quite close to them. They, in turn, kidded him along and told him they knew he was going to be the commanding general of all the Allied Forces in Australia. . . . Yes, and he believed it, which was too bad.[64]

This is in conflict with Brett's claim that Curtin offered supreme command to him, and that he turned it down. It is not unimaginable that MacArthur's perception of Brett's Australian contacts gave rise to this story. By all accounts MacArthur was an exceptionally sensitive man and excessively attentive to his personal destiny. There was no question he was hard to work with. Even Marshall, who respected him, acknowledged MacArthur had to be dealt with carefully: "MacArthur was a very fine commander. He was . . . supersensitive about everything. He thought everybody had ulterior motives about everything. . . . He was conspicuous in the matter of temperament."[65]

MacArthur wasn't the only problem—Sutherland was, according to Gen Rock Brett, "a purebred bastard." Kenney observed that Sutherland was "an arrogant, opinionated, and very ambitious guy. . . . I don't think Sutherland was even loyal to MacArthur. He pretended that he was and I think MacArthur thought he was, but I wouldn't trust him."[66] Sutherland's own stenographer, Paul Rogers, assigns most of the trouble to a flaw in Sutherland's character. In Rogers' words:

> [MacArthur's] behavior falls within the accepted variations allowed any reasonable man in the circumstances of that time and place. He was angry when other reasonable men would have been angry. The expression of his anger fell within the accepted modes of civil discourse. His anger dissipated quickly and was soon forgotten, never intruding into the decision-making process. His will and his intellect were the masters of his emotion. All of this is equally true of Sutherland, with one major failure to understand the impact of pride. . . . Sutherland's career followed the path of Greek tragedy. An initial elevation with MacArthur reached an apogee of pride with a fracturing of personal relations and a final disintegration of his potential.[67]

As complex and difficult as the relationship between MacArthur and Sutherland may have appeared to Gen George Brett, and as tenuous as the supply and personnel situation rendered Allied prospects in the Pacific war, he still was charged with getting the job done. Most of his superiors and many of his subordinates seem to have thought he was not up to the vast administrative and combat challenge facing him. General Smith blamed it on the mixed Australian and American command, "General Brett's mélange was manifestly not going to work."[68] Brett himself clearly thought his staff was weak. Burdette Fitch recalled, "He was a rather easy-going Air Force officer, who was probably a better flier than administrator (as so many of them were)."[69] Kenney even hinted that Brett, in addition to his problems with Sutherland, might have lost his taste for the combat zone.

Sutherland didn't like Brett and Sutherland helped the feud along . . . he helped Brett to continue to dislike MacArthur. I don't think MacArthur really disliked Brett; he just lost confidence in him there.

Brett originally was a damn good supply man back in the States. He ran a good show then. I worked for him there and liked Geroge [sic] Brett very much.

But somehow the kids in New Guinea didn't have confidence in him. He didn't get up there very often; I think he was up there maybe twice. They didn't have much equipment and weren't getting any more equipment; they weren't getting spare parts when their airplanes began falling apart. Brett didn't get them up to them, and he didn't check and find out what they needed and see that they got it. Their food was terrible stuff, and he wouldn't do anything about that. They were getting malaria pretty badly, and there was nothing done about that.

One of the first things I did was introduce flush toilets in New Guinea; he could have done that, but he didn't. He followed the system and followed the rules of Army regulations to the point that he hamstrung himself. You couldn't fight a war by following the rules because your gang would've quit you. Yet you couldn't take care of them unless you broke some rules. . . .

Brett actually told me when I came in to see him when I first got there that he hadn't seen MacArthur for over a month. MacArthur was two floors above him in the same building. When I was there, I wouldn't think of a day going by without going up to see the "Old Man" if there was something I wanted to talk over with him. . . . I wasn't bothered with Sutherland, but when Brett went up there, he would stop at Sutherland's desk to see if MacArthur was in.[70]

By 6 July 1942 Brett's fate had been decided in Washington, and Marshall radioed MacArthur to offer him either Maj Gen George C. Kenney or Brig Gen Jimmy Doolittle as a replacement for Brett. MacArthur selected Kenney because of his continuity of service. The commander in chief predicted Doolittle's long sojourn as a civilian before the war would garner a negative reaction within the Australian air force. On 13 July 1942 MacArthur requested information "as soon as possible" to confirm the replacement of Brett with Kenney. Marshall responded the same day with the following message: "This message to be read by General MacArthur and code clerk only. . . . Orders are being issued today for Kenny [sic] to proceed by air without delay and report to you for assignment and duty. You are authorized to issue necessary orders to return Brett by air to the United States with instructions to report by radio to the adjutant general Washington upon arrival at port of embarkation and await further instructions."[71]

While MacArthur and Marshall were conducting their correspondence regarding Brett's future, Brett was trying to delay the movement of his headquarters from Melbourne to Brisbane. He cited a lack of communications, personnel, and a lack of suitable accommodations as reasons to stay in Melbourne. MacArthur's own headquarters, originally slated to move on 15 July 1942, announced to the War Department on 16 July 1942 that communications were in place and that the General Headquarters would move to Brisbane as of 20 July 1942.[72]

What would not be delayed, however, was MacArthur's determination to replace Brett. As soon as he heard from Marshall, MacArthur informed Brett of his fate:

Personal

Dear Brett:

I have just received a secret directive from General Marshall stating that you are to be replaced here by General Kenney, for whom orders were issued yesterday to proceed by air without delay. I have been directed to issue the necessary orders "to return Brett by air to the United States. . . ." These orders will be issued upon General Kenney's arrival. In order not to inform the enemy that this change of command is taking place, I believe it advisable to keep the matter as secret as possible. Cordially yours, DOUGLAS MacARTHUR[73]

Brett continued to work on issues related to his command, but on 31 July 1942 he wrote the following to General MacArthur: "Subject to your approval and in compliance with written orders for my return to the United States, I am making arrangements to depart from Brisbane on or about the night of August 3rd. Time of departure was determined after conference with General Kenny [sic] regarding his assumption of command. [signed] George H. Brett."[74] On 3 August 1942 Sutherland signed a decoration certifying the award of the Silver Star by General MacArthur to George H. Brett, "For gallantry in action in air reconnaissance in the combat zone, Southwest Pacific Area, during the months of May, June and July, 1942."[75]

General Rock Brett says his father was philosophical about being relieved in Australia. He understood that the war had to be won, and his career aspirations must be subordinated to the overall effort.[76] In his retrospective, however, Gen George Brett evinces a trace of somewhat understandable bitterness, perhaps tinged with revisionism:

> On my way back Stateside, everywhere I went I saw bombers and fighters stacked up waiting to move to Australia. Many had been waiting for a long time. Perhaps some day Washington will explain why they were not moved, when they were so desperately needed. Our effectiveness was curtailed, our losses higher than they should have been, because those men and planes were held back. I was compelled to send into combat fighter pilots with less than ten-hours' experience on the type of plane assigned them, when there were available men with hundreds of hours of flying time in the same type aircraft.
>
> I have my own ideas why this happened, and they reflect little credit on the men involved, but for the moment they must remain only theories.[77]

General Brett remained on duty. He still had important work to do, and his friend George Marshall had a conspicuous assignment for him as the commander of a theater of war. He was to replace Lt Gen Frank Andrews as the senior commander in the Caribbean. As an Airman in command of a theater, he held a unique position. Furthermore, his friendships and contacts with the leadership of Central and South America helped assure the US southern flank would remain quiet throughout the remainder of World War II.

Notes

1. Message, USAFIA, Brett, to Adjutant General of the War Department (AGWAR), 3 March 1942, RG 18, box 1. A war department official reviewing the message underlined the "500–600" enemy aircraft and scrawled a question mark in the margin. The naval figure of "Over 100 transports" was likewise underlined.
2. Pogue, *George C. Marshall*, 250.
3. Rogers, *The Good Years*, 187.
4. Message, USAFIA, Brett, to War Plans Division (WPD), 5 March 1942, RG 18; and Message, USAFIA, Brett, to A-3 , 5 March 1942, RG 18, box 1.
5. Message, USAFIA, Brett, to WPD, 5 March 1942, RG 18, box 1.
6. Message, USAFIA, Brett, to AGWAR, 7 March 1942, RG 18, box 1.
7. Message, USAFIA, Brett, to WPD, 8 March 1942, RG 18, box 1. This message also notes that Brett has been rebuffed in his overtures regarding Dutch participation in the war effort. According to Brett, the Australians insisted the Dutch government must work directly with their prime minister to determine what, if any, role they would play.

8. Message traffic, 8–9 March 1942, General Arnold's Briefs of Messages, 1942–1945, RG 18, boxes 1–3; Message, USAFIA, Brett, to WPD, 9 March 1942, RG 18, box 1.

9. Brett, "The MacArthur I Knew," 28 and 139. The discrepancy between Brett's strength report of a few days earlier listing one B-24 as combat ready and this claim is unexplained.

10. Message, USAFIA, Brett, to WPD, 11 March 1942, RG 18, box 1; Message, USAFIA, Brett, to A-2, 11 March 1942, RG 18, box 1; and Message, USAFIA, Brett, to Air Service Supply, 11 March 1942, RG 18, box 1.

11. Rogers, *The Good Years*, 191. Sutherland sent Godman to see MacArthur, who was impressed with the young man's luck. He added him to his staff as a General Headquarters (GHQ) pilot.

12. Brett, "The MacArthur I Knew," 140.

13. Rogers, *The Good Years*, 192.

14. Brett, "The MacArthur I Knew," 140. Brett had heard from Washington too. On 12 March 1942 he acknowledged a message giving him control of the bombers, and requiring him to use them in support of the Navy: Message, USAFIA, Brett, to WPD, 12 March 1942, RG 18, box 1.

15. Pogue, *George C. Marshall*, 251. Rogers reports that MacArthur had to be coerced into continuing the trip by air. Reports of incoming Japanese bombers increased the staff's urgent desire to get MacArthur traveling again. Rather than mention the potential of an air raid, Sutherland shrewdly used MacArthur's doctor to convince him the road trip would be too hard on young Arthur MacArthur, the general's son, Rogers, *The Good Years*, 193–94. MacArthur himself was reportedly pleased with the performance of the aircrews, and awarded them Silver Stars when they landed south of Darwin. Mrs. MacArthur may have been the source of the trouble. Upon arriving at Batchelor, Australia, she reportedly commented to MacArthur's civilian aide, Sydney Huff, "Never, never again will anybody get me into an airplane! Not for any reason! Sid, please find some way that we can get to Melbourne without getting off the ground." James, *The Years of MacArthur*, 106–7.

16. James, *The Years of MacArthur*, 109.

17. Brett, to the prime minister of Australia, letter, subject: MacArthur's Nomination as Supreme Commander.

18. Brett, "The MacArthur I Knew," 141–42. It might be noted that MacArthur and his family had just traveled over 3,000 miles in very uncomfortable circumstances. Mrs. MacArthur's patience was apparently wearing thin, and their young son was ill from the trip. It is not altogether surprising that MacArthur did not receive Brett the day he arrived in Melbourne. On the other hand, MacArthur did have the energy to send a report to General Marshall that day.

19. Message, MacArthur, to chief of staff, General Marshall, 21 March 1942, Arnold Papers, Library of Congress, Manuscript Division. It is interesting that MacArthur formed such an overwhelmingly negative impression after only brief visits to Batchelor Field and the airfield at Alice Springs. Brett had also clearly developed a relationship with Curtin—it is possible MacArthur was eager to see a rival for political influence removed from the capital city.

20. Message, USAFIA, Brett, to AGWAR, 22 March 1942, RG 18, box 1; Message, USAFIA, Brett, to AGWAR, 21 March 1942, RG 18, box 1.

21. Message, USAFIA, Brett, to A-4, 20 March 1942; RG 18, box 1; Message, USAFIA, Brett, to War Department Organization and Movement (War/ Orig. & Mov't), 23 March 1942, RG 18, box 1.

22. Brett, "The MacArthur I Knew," 142. The disagreement about what happened between MacArthur's staff and Brereton continues to this day, but until the publication of *The Brereton Diaries* MacArthur always publicly praised Brereton's efforts in the Philippines. See Miller, "A 'Pretty Damn Able Commander' Lewis Hyde Brereton: Part II," for more information. Also of note, the friction between MacArthur and Admiral Hart is well documented, and it began long before MacArthur's evacuation from Corregidor. Indeed, MacArthur lays the Philippine defeat at Hart's door, claiming "the crux of the problem lay in the different interpretation given to local problems by Admiral Thomas C. Hart, the naval commander, and myself. . . . Apparently, he was certain that the islands were doomed and made no effort to keep open our lines of supply." See MacArthur, *Reminiscences*, 128; see Rogers, *The Good Years*, 71–76.

23. Brett, "The MacArthur I Knew," 144. In any event Brett never moved his headquarters to Townsville, although he did eventually move to Brisbane. Kenney hints that the comforts of Melbourne may have dampened Brett's offensive spirit; he also pointedly remarks that Brett's house was "one of the best in Brisbane" after his headquarters moved there. Kenney, *General Kenney Reports*, 28, 50, and 79.

24. Message, USAFIA, Brett, to WPD, 25 March 1942, RG 18, box 1; and Message, USAFIA, Brett, to WPD, 27 March 1942, RG 18, box 1. Just below the 28 March 1942 note, in pencil, is the tasking from "HHA" to "Fairchild," directing that the reply be drafted.

25. Message, USAFIA, Brett, to Director of Air Defenses, 29 March 1942, RG 18, box 1.

26. Smith, oral history interview, 35–39. Smith tells of meeting Gen Harold George, an old friend, in the hotel immediately after his interview with Brett. Smith and George talked until late in the night about George's bitter disappointment about being ordered to leave his men in the Philippines. The two journeyed to Brisbane together, where George inspected the assembly depot and provided Smith with his impression that the Japanese would invade Australia. The following day, George departed for Darwin, Australia, where he was tragically killed. In Smith's words: "He had been at Darwin about two hours and was out at the Darwin airstrip watching landings and takeoffs when an Aussie pilot in a P-40 ground looped right into him and killed him, and there goes the fighter commander."

27. Message, USAFIA, Brett, to Marshall, 4 April 1942, RG 18, box 1.

28. Message, USAFFE, MacArthur, to AGWAR, 2 April 1942, box 1.

29. James, *The Years of MacArthur*, 114–16.

30. Message, USAFFE, MacArthur, to AGWAR, 10 April 1942, box 1.

31. Manchester, *American Caesar*, 288; and Message, USAFFE, Brett, to AGWAR, 22 April 1942, RG 18, box 1.

32. Message, USAFFE, Brett, to AGWAR, 22 April 1942, RG 18, box 1.

33. Manchester, *American Caesar*, 289.

34. Message, USAFFE, MacArthur, to OPD, 13 April 1942, RG 18, box 1.

35. Message, USAFFE, Brett, to AGWAR, 18 April 1942, RG 18, box 1; and Message, USAFFE, Brett, to Commanding General Army Air Forces (CG AAF), 19 April 1942, RG 18, box 1.

36. Message, USAFFE, MacArthur, to CG AAF, 22 April 1942, RG 18, box 1. The fact that action to A-1 was directed may indicate Arnold was already preparing for the possibility that Brett might have to be relieved.

37. Message, USAFFE, MacArthur, to CG AAF, 26 April 1942, RG 18, box 1.

38. Message, USAFIA, Brett, to CG AAF, 30 April 1942, RG 18, box 1.

39. Ibid. Brett did eventually arrange to move his headquarters to Brisbane, after he was satisfied the Japanese would not invade the Australian continent. Smith, oral history interview, 51.

40. Message, USAFIA, MacArthur, to Marshall, 1 May 1942, RG 18, box 1.

41. Craven and Cate, *The Army Air Forces in World War II*, 449.

42. Message, Washington, Marshall, to commander in chief, South West Pacific Area (CINC SWPA), 14 May 1942.

43. Brett, Griffith collection, Headquarters United States Army Air Services, *Personnel Report*, 2.

44. Smith, oral history interview, 48.

45. Message, USAFIA, Brett, to CG AAF, 18 May 1942; Message, USAFIA, Brett, to CG AAF, 21 May 1942; and Message, USAFIA, Brett, to CG AAF, 23 May 1942, RG 18, box 2.

46. Message, HQ SWPA, MacArthur, to CG AAF, 24 May 1942, RG 18, box 2.

47. MacArthur, CINC SWPA, to commander, Allied Air Forces, letter, subject: Reprimand for Press Interview, 1 June 1942, MacArthur Memorial.

48. Sutherland, chief of staff, SWPA, to commander, Allied Air Forces, letter, 3 June 1942, subject: Employment of P-39 and P-400 Airplanes; Sutherland, letter, 3 June 1942, subject: Operation of B-17E Airplanes; Fitch, adjutant general, SWPA, letter, 3 June 1942, subject: Decorations, all found in MacArthur Memorial.

49. Sutherland to commander, Allied Air Forces, letter, 4 June 1942, subject: Attacks against Hostile Bomber Concentration in New Britain; and Sutherland to commander, Allied Air Forces, letter, 5 June 1942, subject: Fighter Aircraft, both found in MacArthur Memorial.

50. Bostock, chief of staff, Allied Air Forces SWPA, to chief of staff, SWPA, letter, 5 June 1942, subject: Employment of P-39 and P-400 Aircraft; Bostock to chief of staff, SWPA, letter, 5 June 1942, subject: Attacks against hostile Bomber Concentration in New Britain, both found in MacArthur Memorial.

51. Brett, commander, Allied Air Forces SWPA, to CINC SWPA, letter, 9 June 1942, subject: Public Relations; MacArthur, CINC SWPA, to commander, Allied Air Forces, letter, 10 June 1942, subject, Public Relations, 10 June 1942, both found in MacArthur Memorial. One suspects MacArthur's implication in his final line is that US forces, at least the Air Force, had yet to accomplish anything.

52. General, US Army, commander in chief, to commander, Allied Air Forces, letter, 10 June 1942, subject: Attacks against Hostile Bomber Concentration in New Britain, MacArthur Memorial.

53. George H. Brett, commander, Allied Air Forces SWPA, to CINC SWPA, letter, 11 June 1942, subject: Attacks against Hostile Bomber Concentrations in New Britain, MacArthur Memorial.

54. Fitch, adjutant general SWPA, to commander, Allied Air Forces, letter, 13 June 1942, subject, Air Transport for General Headquarters, MacArthur Memorial.

55. Bostock to CINC SWPA, letter, 14 June 1942, subject: Air Transport for General Headquarters; Fitch to commander, Allied Air Forces, letter, 16 June 1942, subject: Air Transport for General Headquarters; Godman, General Headquarters pilot, to adjutant general, SWPA, memorandum, subject, B-17C 02072, undated, all found in MacArthur Memorial. Brett later castigated Godman privately to Kenney, remarking "Captain Godman, of the Air Corps, who is Aide to General Sutherland, has a very poor reputation among his own branch of the service. Sutherland is said to seek his advice on G.H.Q. decisions regarding the Air Forces." Brett, Lt Gen George H. "Comments of Gen. Brett".

56. Sutherland to commander, Allied Air Forces, letter, 20 June 1942, subject: Reconnaissance, MacArthur Memorial.

57. Message, GHQ SWPA, MacArthur, to AGWAR, 18 June 1942, RG 18, box 2.

58. Message, GHQ SWPA, Brett, to CG AAF, 19 June 1942; Messages, GHQ SWPA, Brett, to Air Services Command, 25 June 1942, RG 18, box 2.

59. Message, GHQ SWPA, MacArthur, to Plans, 26 June 1942, RG 18, box 2.

60. Message, chief of staff, War Department, Marshall, to CINC SWPA, 29 June 1942.

61. Green, "Prelude to Pearl Harbor Attack."

62. Green, collection.

63. Message, GHQ SWPA, MacArthur, to Marshall, 30 June 1942.

64. Kenney, "Oral Reminiscences of General George C. Kenney," 13 and 15.

65. Pogue, *George C. Marshall*, 374–75. At least part of Brett's story, the fact that he was offered command, can be confirmed. On 28 February 1942 the combined Australian and New Zealand chiefs of staff "advised that a Supreme Commander, preferably an American, should be appointed. . . . This proposal was sent to Churchill to be passed on to Roosevelt. Australia indicated that the appointment as Supreme Commander of Lieut-General George H. Brett, then commanding the American troops in Australia, would be welcomed." Gavin Long, *The Six Years War*, 174.

66. Manchester, *American Caesar*, 302–3.

67. Rogers, *The Good Years*.

68. Smith, oral history interview, 50.

69. Fitch, "Oral Reminiscences of Brigadier General Burdette M. Fitch," 2. Although one might suspect Fitch of being tainted by association with MacArthur since he was the adjutant general, he actually served with Brett first in

Java. MacArthur selected Fitch for his staff after MacArthur's arrival in Melbourne.

70. Kenney, "Oral Reminiscences of General George C. Kenney," 16–17.

71. Message, chief of staff, War Department, Marshall, to CINC SWPA, 6 July 1942; Message, CINC SWPA, MacArthur, to Marshall, 7 July 1942; Message, CINC SWPA, MacArthur, to chief of staff, War Department, 13 July 1942; Message, chief of staff, War Department, Marshall, to CINC SWPA, 13 July 1942, RG 18, box 2.

72. Brett, commander, Allied Air Forces SWPA, to CINC SWPA, letter, 5 July 1942, subject: Allied Air Forces Headquarters Move from Melbourne to Brisbane, MacArthur Memorial.

73. MacArthur, CINC SWPA, to commander, Allied Air Forces, letter, 14 July 1942, subject: Change of Command, MacArthur Memorial.

74. Brett to CINC SWPA, letter, 31 July 1942, subject: Departure from Australia, MacArthur Memorial.

75. Sutherland, chief of staff, SWPA, order, subject: Award of Silver Star, 3 August 1942, MacArthur Memorial.

76. Brett, interview by the author, 11 February 2004.

77. Brett, "The MacArthur I Knew," 149.

Chapter 6

Command in the Caribbean

At the beginning of August 1942 Gen George Brett received permission from MacArthur's staff to depart Australia in his adopted plane, the B-17, known as the *Swoose*. The *Swoose* left Australia on 4 August 1942 and flew via Hickam Field, Hawaii, to Hamilton Field, north of San Francisco, landing there on 7 August 1942. The aircraft was in the air 36 hours and 10 minutes, setting a speed record for a flight from Australia to the continental United States. The return trip was also unusual because the *Swoose* was the first bomber to return to the United States after a combat tour. Mrs. Mary Devol Brett boarded the B-17 in San Francisco for the trip to Washington, DC. The bomber arrived there on 12 August 1942.[1]

Just before he landed in Washington, DC, Brett had been heralded for his leadership, affability, and flying skill in the 8 August 1942 issue of *Collier's*.[2] On 22 August 1942, General Brett gave an address to AAF technical training graduates in Miami. Brett's appearance was kept secret until he strode onto the stage. Addressing the ground officers, Brett offered a grimly realistic appraisal of the challenge awaiting them in the theater of war: "The fighting is absolutely dependent upon the ground. . . . You carry the load. It is a thankless job with no glory and no glamour [*sic*]. You will be met by a confused mass of inefficiency in some of the theaters to which you may be assigned. Australia has four different gauge railroads in traveling a distance of 1,600 miles. The difficulty of supply increases many fold when you consider that your source is 6,000 miles away and the receipt of the average shipment takes from a month to six weeks."[3]

This first public appearance in the United States preceded the announcement in mid-September 1942 that Kenney had replaced Brett in the Southwest Pacific area. At the end of August Brett began a public tour of the United States to spread lessons learned in the Pacific war to industrial and military organizations across the country. This trip lasted until the end of

September, when the *Swoose* returned to Bolling Field, Washington, DC, to be extensively refurbished.[4]

While he was in Washington, Brett had a fateful interview with General Marshall. According to Gen Rock Brett, his dad was expecting a court-martial associated with his relief in Australia upon his return to the United States. Marshall soon calmed this fear. Indeed, the chief of staff asked Brett not to demand a court-martial because of the negative publicity it would cause. Offering him an assignment as the commander of the Caribbean Defense Command, Marshall urged his friend to keep quiet about his frustrations, and Brett compliantly accepted the job. Marshall reportedly told Brett: "I'm not writing any . . . books when this is over, and I hope you won't either."[5]

Although Brett's future had been decided, it had not yet been announced to a news-hungry public. As a high-ranking warrior on a tour of the country, Brett became somewhat famous. The Associated Press carried several stories about him, to include an article touting the award of the Distinguished Flying Cross to General Brett for his "heroism and extraordinary achievement while participating in aerial flights from September, 1941, to September, 1942." On 3 November 1942 the *New York Daily News* carried a story picturing Brett at the controls of a bomber, decorating troops in Australia, and sleeping "in the radio room" of a B-17 in flight.[6]

At the end of September an article appeared in the *Washington Times Herald* intimating that General Brett would replace General Arnold and that Arnold would be sent to England. This report was heartily denied at a press conference given by Secretary of War Henry L. Stimson on 24 September 1942. The report appeared roughly one week after General Arnold had departed Washington, DC, for a tour of the Pacific theater during which he paid a visit to Brett's successor in Australia, General Kenney. Brett was not fated to stay in Washington, however on 6 November 1942 the *Swoose* left Bolling Field en route to Albrook Field, Panama, via Miami, Florida. Arriving in the wee hours of 9 November 1942, Brett and his crew climbed out of their well-traveled warhorse and into the moist Panamanian night.[7]

Replacing his close friend, Lt Gen Frank M. Andrews, Brett was assuming command of the recently inaugurated Caribbean Defense Command, an organization responsible for the defense of the Panama Canal Zone and US interests in Central and South America. Established as the Panama Canal Department in 1917, during Brett's tenure the command made its headquarters at Quarry Heights, a US military installation constructed in 1911. With operational responsibility for all ground, air, and naval activity in his area of operations, General Brett assumed command at the peak of a buildup that counted 68,000 defenders by the beginning of 1943. Control was exercised through a joint operations center that had been established earlier in 1942.[8]

By 12 November 1942 Brett was in command, and on that day he sent a message to the director of bombardment in Washington, DC, outlining a plan for the rotation of heavy bomber squadrons out of the Caribbean area. In the dispatch he described the mission impact of relieving the bombardment squadrons too soon: "Training is at a minimum and all efforts are being directed at Axis submarines and it is believed advisable to defer the exchange of medium bombardment groups until these groups have full equipment of airplanes and combat crews adequately trained as the relief of one medium squadron would reduce anti-submarine work by twenty-five percent. It is further recommended that exchange be extended to include fighter squadrons."[9] Eight days later Brett had discovered another deficiency within his new command. Recognition procedures preventing friendly aircraft from firing on friendly surface vessels were not coordinated with procedures in the adjoining Pacific theater. "Urgently recommend that recognition procedure for the PACIFIC theater be extended immediately to include this area." Between these messages to Washington, Brett made a flying-tour inspection of his new command.[10]

At the beginning of December Brett received a shock. Ten to 20 enemy vessels were "435 miles southwest of San Francisco." Brett urgently requested an update because the local press reported the intelligence warning was a mistake, which it apparently was. After Christmas 1942 Brett penned an interesting letter to his friend and boss, Lt Gen Henry H. Arnold. In it he praises Arnold's leadership, briefly contemplating his experience of the war so far.

Dear Hap:

The past has been difficult up and down, and back and forth, but all things appear to be smoothing out, and as a result of your most capable leadership and dynamic personality, reports from all over the world indicate a growing ascendancy of the Army Air Forces.

May I wish you all the success in the coming year and increased accomplishments resulting from the study and application of basic principles. I still maintain you can never get water out of a nozzle and hose unless you have a . . . good pump somewhere in the background.

Sincerely Yours,

George H. Brett,
Lieutenant General, U.S. Army

The last paragraph of the note could be subjected to numerous interpretations, but since it is written from the perspective of a supply officer, perhaps it is meant to focus Arnold's concentration on logistical issues. Wishing one's superior officer success through "study and application of basic principles" seems like a left-handed compliment at best, but as observed above, Brett's writing style was often murky. It is difficult to judge exactly what he meant by the phrase.[11]

On the next day Brett demonstrated his typical level of involvement in logistical matters. He sent a message to the services of supply attempting to coordinate the shipment of "[o]ne million three hundred thousand gallons of cutback asphalt" from the Canal Zone to the Galapagos Islands for the construction of an airfield there. He suggested co-opting two small inbound oil tankers for the job or one large oil tanker on a regular route between Aruba and Panama. Although Brett probably enjoyed the opportunity to work on logistical issues, his primary job in Panama was as Washington, DC's, representative to Central and South America. He traveled extensively, making contacts with senior Latin American military officials in hopes of stemming some of the pro-German feeling in the region.[12]

One benefit of being closer to home was more regular contact with his family. In the summer of 1942, Brett sent some pictures to General Arnold for him to pass along to Mary Devol Brett in Miami Beach. Arnold wrote: "Just received the attached pictures from George. I have talked to several people who have come back from that theatre [sic], and apparently he is in fine shape." In the summer of 1943, Brett would actually receive a visit from a

Lt Gen George H. Brett, commander, Caribbean Defense Command

group of US Military Academy cadets, one of whom was his son Rock. In between, the general spent most of his time flying to the far-flung parts of his theater, offering the services of his aircraft to local military, government, and even medical officials. Brett reportedly let the presidents of Cuba and Nicaragua fly as copilots of the *Swoose* during "good neighbor" visits.[13]

The May 1943 *Air Force Journal* carried a feature by Capt Charles D. Frazer, describing the military mission in the Antilles as defensive, conducted by AAF fighters, and offensive, conducted by bombers, Navy aircraft, and surface vessels. According to Frazer, "Bombardment squadrons are organized to hunt U-boats. This is the most important function of the Antilles Air Task Force, since the submarine is a vicious, ever-present menace to shipping through the Caribbean. Subs have even shelled some of the islands. . . . The large fields in the Caribbean area serve also as important way stations for the Air Transport Command and through them passes the greatest volume of military air traffic of any region in the world."[14]

Brett's command was frequently visited by a bevy of dignitaries, both military and civilian, who regularly rubbed shoulders with the more plebeian masses stationed in the area. Frazer gives an atmospheric description of the Officer's Club bar, Borinquen Field, Puerto Rico:

> Elbowing and shoving their way up democratically for a rum-coke or a daiquiri may be seen foreign diplomats and military aides, ferry pilots and war correspondents, "brass hats" of all the United Nations and ordinary seamen—survivors of torpedoed ships—dressed in the garb of the rescued sailor, a cheap seersucker suit.
>
> . . . Combat and ferry pilots of the Army Air Forces mingle with flyers from Britain, the Netherlands, Free France, China, Russia, and many other nations. Prominent in the crowd will always be the gay and vivacious airmen of Latin America.
>
> Not all celebrities are uniformed, by any means. A sombre business suit may call attention to a Wendell Willkie or a screen actor on U.S.O. tour or other globe-trotters, en route to or from the States.[15]

The flight log of the *Swoose* records that Brett visited Miami; the island nation of Trinidad; Quito, Ecuador; San Juan, Puerto Rico; San Jose, Costa Rica; Bogotá, Colombia; Santiago, Chile; and Lima, Peru, between December 1942 and June 1943. In July 1943 Brett took famous journalist Lowell Thomas on an aerial inspection tour of the Panama Canal fortifications. According to a former *Swoose* pilot, Brett's favorite way to close a visit was with a low, high-speed pass over the airfield on departure.[16]

In the whirl of constant travel and frequent entertainment for dignitaries of various cultures and languages, there were ample opportunities for misunderstanding. By winter 1943 the *Swoose* was beginning to show its age, with wing and fuselage corrosion threatening to scrap the aircraft. Capt Jack J. Crane, the *Swoose* pilot at that time, knew of Brett's emotional attachment to the aircraft, and went out of his way to find a way to save it. Searching a storage shed at France Field, he discovered "two new B-17B inboard wing panels" which apparently had been lost or abandoned. "General Brett was delighted by Crane's discovery. The deal soon was consummated with the depot's commanding officer, a Colonel Munro, to begin the overhaul of the *Swoose* on a low-priority basis, relative to other essential work at the depot. Plans also were made to update the *Swoose* to B-17E standards wherever practical."[17]

Not completed until 30 May 1944, Crane described the reinvigorated *Swoose* as "a true queen of the skies." The extensive renovation of the *Swoose* became the partial basis of an inspector general complaint leveled against Brett. His entertainment of dignitaries also must have included boat or fishing trips, since part of the complaint alleges Brett "converted an AAF Rescue Boat into a private yacht at a cost of $88,000–$225,000." Initiated by General Marshall 16 months after the repair of the *Swoose* had been completed, the investigation charged Brett with "expend[ing] over $200,000 to convert a B-17 bomber into a luxury liner and with having had miniatures of that airplane, known as the 'Swoose' manufactured at Government expense, to be used as gifts for friends." The accusations continued:

> Still other allegations charge that the 12th AAF Emergency Rescue Boat Squadron and its equipment were used primarily for fishing parties for senior officers; that spoilage of food valued at $100,000 was not covered by a report of survey; that furniture was manufactured by the Panama Air Depot at Government expense for various officers and that as a result of these extravagances employees of the Panama Air Depot struck and they, as well as employees of the Panama Canal, cancelled [sic] their War Bond subscriptions.[18]

If the allegations against General Brett were true they were not substantiated by the inspector general's report. The inspector general, Lt Gen Dan I. Sultan, reported to Marshall on 23 November 1945 that most of the charges were, in fact, distortions of mission-related events and expenditures, and that "the remaining allegations were found to be without a basis in fact. . . . I concur in the reporting officer's recommendation that no further action be taken in this matter." One interesting tidbit from Brett's previous tour in Panama might be interpreted as a somewhat more relaxed attitude toward government resources than the carefully enforced separation of personal and government business that exists by today's regulations. In a letter to a friend at the Virginia Military Institute on 19 March 1938, Brett describes his plans to visit a VMI graduate in Aruba with the following words, "By the way, there was a man by the name of Harrison, along in the class of about 14 or 15, around your time, who is now one of the managing directors of a big oil company on a little island called Aruba, approximately eight hundred miles east of Panama and just off the north coast of Central America. I am planning to take about twenty airplanes over there the latter part of April and have ourselves a good time."[19] On the other hand, Brett could also be taken to refer merely to the fun of leading an exciting flight mission to a tropical destination, which was, after all, his job.

By the time General Sultan cleared Brett of any wrongdoing his career in the AAF was already at an end. On 21 February 1945 Brett had requested voluntary retirement as of 30 May 1945, "the date upon which I will have completed 4 years detail as Chief of the Army Air Corps." In the request letter he certifies that he is "not under investigation." On 30 April 1945 Brett retired as a major general, and on 1 May 1945 returned to active duty "without interruption in his capacity and office as a temporary lieutenant general, AUS, and as Commanding General of the Caribbean Defense Command and Panama Canal Department."[20]

In June 1945 the *Swoose* served as transportation for General Brett and a Latin American delegation from Panama to San Francisco, where the charter of the United Nations was signed. After one final trip to Santiago, Chile, in September 1945, Brett was relieved by Lt Gen Willis D. Crittenberger on 10 October 1945. On 15 October 1945 Brett departed from Panama aboard the *Swoose*, farewelled on the flight line by troops who were treated to a final low-level, high-speed pass by General Brett after the aircraft took off. Arriving in San Antonio, Texas, on 17 October 1945, the *Swoose* began a series of stops that traversed the United States from California to Florida, Washington, DC, to Albuquerque, New Mexico. General Brett used the *Swoose* as his personal aircraft until 1 December 1945, when he flew it on a mission between Kirtland AFB, New Mexico, and

Los Angeles. That same month the aircraft was retired to Kingman Army Air Field, Arizona. General Brett's instructions were that the nose art be removed from the aircraft so that its history would not be exploited after the war, but this directive was never carried out.[21]

As Brett was concluding his career, the War Department awarded him with his second Distinguished Service Medal for his service in Panama. The citation celebrates "his broad grasp of military strategy and superior knowledge of air and ground tactics" and depicts the importance of his contributions to international relations. "He succeeded admirably in impressing the republics of Central and South America with the importance and necessity of hemispheric solidarity, imbued them with American ideals, coordinated their use of arms and equipment and indoctrinated them with American training methods—all of which fostered continued improvement in the relations between all America republics."[22] His record also notes he spent time as a patient in Brooke General Hospital, Texas, after his temporary duty in Albuquerque, New Mexico, and Miami, Florida. Treated for a heart condition, he was released from the hospital in April 1946, and assigned to the Fort Sam Houston Separation Center, Texas, for administrative purposes until he reverted to retired status on 10 May 1946.[23]

On 23 May 1946 the new commanding general of the AAF, Gen Carl Spaatz, sent a personal letter of thanks to the retiring general:

Dear Brett:

As you lay down the heavy responsibilities which you have carried so long, I want to express some measure of our gratitude for the capable assistance you have given to the Army Air Forces during your many years of active service.

Your military career has been marked with a high degree of leadership and devotion to duty which has enabled you to render service of distinction and of great value to the Allied Nations. Especially noteworthy is the effective manner in which you administered your duties as Commander of the Allied Air Forces in the South West Pacific Theater, and as Commanding General of the Caribbean Defense Command. You were well qualified to fulfill the exacting requirements of those important assignments, and through your cooperativeness, and tenacity of purpose you set, and adhered to, a high standard of accomplishment for your Commands. Your courage and calm fortitude have earned you the devotion and respect of all familiar with your outstanding achievements.

We are indeed grateful for your exemplary performance of military duties, and I sincerely hope that your life of retirement will be filled with a world of happiness.

Very sincerely,

CARL SPAATZ
General, U. S. Army
Commanding General, Army Air Forces[24]

Brett was advanced to the grade of lieutenant general on the USAF retired list by an Act of Congress, 29 June 1948.[25]

In his retirement years, Brett turned to writing. In October 1947 Brett penned a *True Magazine* article, "The MacArthur I Knew." In 1952 he co-wrote *The Air Force Officer's Guide* with Albert Douglas. In February 1948 he sent a copy of a speech he delivered to students of the "Tactical School" to General Spaatz. The speech explores the topic of moral leadership, encouraging the young officers in the audience to succeed through integrity, introspection, loyalty, responsibility, and self-control. The letterhead Brett used in corresponding with Spaatz shows he was employed by the Lincoln National Life Insurance Company in Winter Park, Florida. Brett spent some of his energy trying to help Airmen understand the value of life insurance. The Air University Library, Maxwell AFB, Alabama, contains a paper he wrote entitled "Life Insurance and its Application to Air Force Officers." Rock Brett says his father was heavily influenced in this enterprise by the loss of many pilots during the Air Corps's disastrous attempt to deliver airmail in the period following World War I. These young men left widows and orphans with no one to care for them.[26]

Retirement years left General Brett more time for family and charitable pursuits. His son gratefully recalled his father's kindness when the young man returned from occupation duty in Europe with an Austrian wife: his mother and father reached out to their foreign-born daughter-in-law. Rock Brett soon deployed to the Korean War and George Brett took his daughter-in-law and grandchild in and cared for them to the great relief of the young fighter pilot. Gen George Brett also devoted much of his time to the improvement of the nascent Air Force, participating as a member of the Flying Pay Board and the Air Force Association Board. His work as a board member allowed the retired general to make plans to go back overseas, and he wrote to the Directorate of military personnel in the Pentagon to request information on making arrangements for official travel to Panama, England, France, Germany, and "maybe Spain."[27]

Gen George H. Brett's hard work eventually ended. On 2 December 1963 at the age of 77, he succumbed to cancer while in the hospital at Orlando AFB, Florida. Brett was survived by his wife, children, and grandchildren.[28] Private and public tributes quickly followed Brett's death. The *Washington Post* ran a quarter-page obituary describing his many career accomplishments, including his distinguished service on the President's Service Academy Board of 1949–50. Rep. Edward J. Gurney of Florida's 11th District entered the *Post*'s report into the *Congressional Record* on 12 December 1963, and on 23 March 1964 Senator Spessard L. Holland of Florida remembered Brett as "a dedicated soldier and a great American who served his country well." The senator entered the eulogy presented at Brett's funeral into the *Congressional Record* on 23 March 1964. The eulogy was given by then-Lt Col Rock Brett, and his words reflect the high admiration he felt for his father:

> His role as a father, a grandfather, and in this his last year as a great grandfather, won him no medals, but no man was a finer father to his children nor ever did more to weld together a deep sense of family love and devotion—one that will certainly last through many generations. His every action had in it a purpose for their well-being. From the home on the lake, which was for their pleasure, to the stern lectures which were to make them more useful citizens, his love for them shone through like a beacon. On his very last day his thoughts and few difficult words concerned the Air Force Academy ambitions of two of his grandsons. His were words of advice. So even as death was near—which he knew but ignored —his great love prevailed over the thoughts of his own discomfort.
>
> His appreciation of and devotion to his many wonderful friends, of all ages and walks of life, made his life a constant pleasure, both to himself and those who surrounded him.[29]

Notes

1. Brownstein, *The Swoose*, 100–101. According to Brownstein, Gen Hap Arnold beat the record by 17 minutes in a C-87 in October of that same year.
2. Courtney, "Born to Fly," 13 and 38–39.
3. Associated Press, *Hard Work Ahead of New Officers.*
4. Brownstein, *The Swoose*, 101–2.
5. Brett, interview by the author, 3 December 2003.

6. Associated Press, "General Brett Is Awarded Flying Cross."

7. Green, "Prelude to Pearl Harbor Attack;" and Brownstein, *The Swoose*, 103. Green theorizes in a handwritten note that the story of Arnold's replacement was fabricated and leaked to the press by Brett.

8. Copp, *Frank M. Andrews*, 21; and "US Southern Command History."

9. Message, Caribbean Defense Command (CDC), Brett, to Director of Bombardment, 12 November 1942, RG 18, box 3.

10. Message, CDC, Brett, to Director of Communications, 20 November 1942, RG 18, box 3; and Brownstein, *The Swoose*, 104.

11. Message, CDC, Brett, to G-2, 4 December 1942, RG 18, box 3; and Arnold, "Correspondence (General)," n.p.

12. Message, CDC, Brett, to Services of Supply (SOS), 31 December 1942, RG 18, box 3; and Brownstein, *The Swoose*, 105.

13. Message, CDC, Brett, to G-2, 4 December 1942, RG 18, box 3; Arnold, "Correspondence (General)," n.p.; and Brownstein, *The Swoose*, 106. According to Brownstein, Cuban president Fulgencio Batista and Nicaraguan president Anastasio Somoza both got the chance to fly the *Swoose* for 15 minutes, trying out a few maneuvers under the watchful eye of the general.

14. Frazer, "Notes from the Antilles," RG 18, box 7.

15. Ibid.

16. Brownstein, *The Swoose*, 106.

17. Ibid., 110–11.

18. Military Record, Memorandum, Sultan, Inspector General to Marshall, chief of staff, subject: Misuse of AAF Rescue Boats and Other Irregularities, 23 November 1945.

19. Ibid. See also Brett, Brig Gen George H., to Lt Col Burress, letter.

20. See both of the following citations in Military Record, Brett, commander, CDC, to Adjutant General, Washington, DC, letter, subject: Application for Voluntary Retirement; Berry, deputy assistant chief of staff, G-1, to Marshall, chief of staff, memorandum, subject: Relief from Active Duty of Lieutenant General George H. Brett.

21. Brownstein, *The Swoose*, 114 and 118–21; Military Record, Berry, deputy assistant chief of staff, G-1, memorandum to Marshall, chief of staff, subject: Relief from Active Duty of Lieutenant General George H. Brett. Brownstein reports the *Swoose* was also used by Brett's son-in-law, then-Col Bernard A. Schriever, for a few days in October to fly between northern and southern California.

22. Military Record, War Department, *Citation for Distinguished Service Medal, Oak Leaf Cluster, Lieutenant General George H. Brett*, 4 December 1945.

23. Colonel Judge, Air Adjutant general, memorandum, subject: Statement of Military Service, 15 March 1949; US Veterans Administration, *Request for Information*, 13 March 1958.

24. Military Record, Spaatz, commanding general, AAF, to Brett, letter, subject: Retirement, 23 May 1946.

25. Military Record, US Air Force, DD Form 13.

26. *Air University Libraries Catalog*; Brett, Lincoln National Life Insurance Company, to chief of staff, United States Air Force, letter, subject: Moral Leadership Talk, 8 February 1948; and Brett, interview by the author.

27. Brett, interview by the author; Brett, Air Force board member, to Sliker, Directorate Military Personnel, letter, Subject: Overseas Official Travel, 15 January 1956.

28. Military Record, US DD Form 1300: *Report of Casualty*, 4 December 1963. The cause of death is annotated as "tracheal obstruction, due to bronchogenic carcinoma."

29. All citations collected by Virginia Military Institute, obituary, "General Brett, Fought 2 Wars;" *Congressional Record*—Appendix, *Gen. George H. Brett*, 12 December 1963; *Congressional Record*—Appendix, *Eulogy of Lt. Gen. George Howard Brett*, 23 March 1964.

Chapter 7

Conclusion

This book developed a picture of Gen George H. Brett that allows an examination of his leadership and combat execution. The analysis of archival materials and anecdotes enabled a broader understanding of his life, character, and some of the challenges he faced, particularly during the early years of World War II in the Pacific theater. The portrait of a hard-working, patriotic leader has emerged from the historical record, but Brett was not perfect, and the question to be answered here is whether his imperfections prevented him from achieving his mission in Australia. There can be little dispute that the circumstances of his command were very harsh indeed, and the obstacles he had to surmount were great. Did Brett do the best anyone could have done, given the hand he was dealt? Did he make any missteps that led to his eventual relief and replacement by Maj Gen George C. Kenney, or was he merely the victim of personal enmity from General Sutherland and the misunderstanding of air force operations by General MacArthur?

Two methods will be used to explore these questions. First, Brett will be measured against Forrest C. Pogue's eight characteristics of George Marshall's old-fashioned leadership. Brett exemplified many of them, but others seem to have eluded him to some extent. Particularly, self-certainty, simplicity of spirit, and loyalty were points of some difficulty for Brett. Whether his response to these leadership challenges resulted more from his character and motivation or more from his circumstances will be clarified by a second method of analysis. Specifically, Brett's combat execution was looked at through the lens of what he knew about employing airpower. This knowledge includes contemporary airpower doctrine, but also measures how flexible Brett was in finding solutions to situations where doctrine fell short or proved to be simply wrong. The historical record indicates that Brett was well versed in the hows and whys of airpower, and that he employed his scarce resources to good effect on numerous occasions. Tricky problems spawned in the dark doctrinal corners of peacetime are cast into sharp relief by the relentless glare of combat. Brett's aptitude for finding solutions to these problems was uneven, and it is in this area that he probably suffered most. Indeed, his attempt to handle cooperation with the Royal Australian Air Force through a mingled command structure from top to bottom of the Allied air forces counts as his most serious mistake.

Brett gave a very strong showing on many of Pogue's leadership characteristics (see table 1). He was quick to pick up on problems, and he didn't hesitate to become involved in solving them. MacArthur described him as "naturally . . . brilliantly gifted." His attention to the concerns of his command throughout the war shows the ability to learn and to translate his perceptions into action. His sense of duty was relentless, and he drove himself hard with a merciless travel schedule at the beginning of the war and during his days in command of the Caribbean Defense Command. During his tenure in Melbourne he dispatched voluminous message traffic to Washington, DC, covering a plethora of subjects and indicating an impressive grasp of the details inherent in the operations of the Allied air forces. In his negative evaluation MacArthur compliments Brett on his energy, calling him an "unusually hard worker."

Brett's sense of duty also extended to his attitude in adversity. Although he hoped to take command of the combat air forces upon his arrival in the Pacific, he was initially assigned

Table 1. Gen George H. Brett's leadership performance

Pogue's Leadership Criteria	Brett's Performance
1. Self-certainty (Experience, Discipline)	Qualified
2. Ability to Learn	Yes
3. Sense of Duty	Yes
4. Acceptance of Responsibility	Yes
5. Simplicity of Spirit	Qualified
6. Character	Qualified
7. Loyalty	Qualified
8. Compassion	Yes

command of the United States Army Forces in Australia, which was envisioned as a combat support organization. General Brereton tells how Brett conducted a conference to determine how best to support Brereton's effort in the north. "In spite of his disappointment at not assuming command of the air force, General Brett was perfectly splendid. . . . His attitude and actions could not have been more helpful. He had a reputation of being a 'tough egg,' but I never saw that side of him."[1] Later Brett turned down the chance to take the air force command in the American British Dutch and Australian Command because he had already promised General Wavell he would be deputy commander of the ill-fated organization.

Such an action demonstrates Brett's willingness to accept responsibility, even when the challenge was an unpleasant one. It is very unlikely Brett was not aware of the long odds facing ABDACOM. His own aircraft had barely escaped destruction on a friendly airfield through a last-minute flight under emergency conditions. When he continued his mission in Australia, it appeared to him and his hosts that the Japanese would soon invade the southern continent. Despite a very daunting task of preparing Australia to resist and ultimately become the stepping-stone to victory, Brett did not hesitate. His transmissions to Washington, DC, portray the unvarnished challenge insistently and repeatedly, but they never betray weariness or resignation. Brett was always pushing for more troops, more planes, and more capable officers to get the mission done.

This firm approach to the problem speaks to his character. *Merriam-Webster* defines character in this vein as "moral excellence and firmness."[2] There is no hint anywhere in the historical documents examined for this book, nor in the commentary of his contemporaries, that anyone had doubts about Brett's moral excellence. His success as a husband and father despite the heavy burdens levied on him throughout his career is testament to his moral fiber—he succeeded where many other prominent men failed. As for his firmness, Brett was well known for standing unwaveringly for what he believed. When he discovered that his son was temporarily in trouble at West Point he sagely advised him to take his lumps, offering neither consolation nor assistance, asking only "Are you going to make it?"[3] Character is a term with different definitions for different people, however. In a 1973 interview Gen Earle Partridge was asked about George Brett, and his conclusion was quite different: "Q: How about George Brett? He was a comer; all of a sudden, his star faded? P: I knew him very well. I'm not at all surprised that he faded away. I liked him very much. I liked to serve with him. But he didn't have the strength of character that was required for high ranking wartime officers. He got in trouble with MacArthur. He got sent back. I wouldn't be surprised."[4] Unfortunately, Partridge's definition of strength of character required for high-ranking wartime officers is not included in the interview.

Partridge's profession of his affection for Brett, however, is echoed by most who knew him. MacArthur called his personality "delightful," and he remained close to Arnold until the latter's death, despite their professional differences. This can be attributed to his evident compassion, especially for his subordinates. In his article "The MacArthur I Knew," Brett recalls the heroism and sacrifice of the Airmen under his command with deep emotion. To the end of his life, Brett put family before himself; the story of his devotion to his Austrian daughter-in-law and her young son is a poignant example of this quality.

The first leadership criteria, however, is great self-certainty borne of experience and self-discipline. While Brett's firmness is discussed above, it was not necessarily synonymous with self-certainty. Brett himself faults his experience in aerial operations as the commander of Crissy Field, but later appraisals of his flying skill point to his proficiency. His experience in direct command of troops and fliers was counted as successful by Arnold, although his performance in high command received a negative appraisal from the secretary of war. Self-discipline was also sometimes a weak point, as some of his evaluations from the First World War show.

Brett's ratings, especially once he became a general officer, indicated a degree of stubbornness and inflexibility that made it difficult for other forceful personalities to work with him easily. The general officer evaluation form of the time pointedly asks, "Does he render willing and generous support to the plans of his superiors regardless of his personal views in the matter?" For Arnold at least, the answer to this question was problematic in Brett's case. He described Brett as sometimes allowing his own viewpoint to take precedence over his loyal support for his superiors.

This inflexible attitude became a burden to Brett during the war years. Arnold was particularly concerned that Brett would exceed his mandate during his trip to England before the war began, and he was reportedly angered by Brett's extremely pessimistic assessment of the possibility of bombing Japan from China. In a memorandum to the War Plans Division on 31 December 1941, Arnold complained "the job given Brett was to determine the way to bomb Japan from China with heavy bombers. He was not given the job to determine ways and means for *not* doing it. The attached is a cable full of 'nots.' I want to find out how to do, not how not to do it" (emphasis in original). By contrast, Chennault's overly optimistic assessment was also of very little use to the AAF chief.[5]

Brett's capacity for hardheadedness sometimes crossed over into pride, a failing which violated the leadership criteria described as simplicity of spirit. Kenney claimed that Brett had aspirations for supreme command in Australia and that he pursued political constituencies in that country to secure the job. MacArthur perceived, perhaps incorrectly, that Brett was jealous of the older general's appointment to the post, and accused Brett of "more or less harmless intrigues." Some of Brett's contemporaries and subordinates in the Air Corps had the impression that he saw himself as struggling with Arnold for the service's top post, deputy chief of staff for air.[6] While there was no question that Brett was ambitious, this characteristic is probably as important to high command as intellect and energy. There is no way to substantiate allegations that Brett actively opposed Arnold and, based on his acknowledged character, it seems unlikely that he did anything underhanded.

Whatever Brett did to create the impression among members of the Air Corps that he wanted Arnold's job, similar behavior may be responsible for MacArthur's intuition that Brett's envy would make him a disloyal subordinate, or worse, a potential political rival. While Brett's passionate description of the brave Airmen under his command shows his loyalty to his subordinates, his loyalty to his superiors was occasionally suspect, at least according to the efficiency reports quoted above. Brett was inclined to avoid or delay orders he did not think served the interest of the troops and fliers under his command. While there is no indication he ignored orders for personal reasons, his paper dispute with Sutherland is an obvious example of Brett's capacity to elude the commander's wishes. MacArthur describes his professional behavior as "evasive," and Kenney expressed shock at the notion that Brett had not seen MacArthur in person for a period of weeks.

In his written debrief to Kenney, Brett slammed MacArthur and the GHQ staff. Claiming to have seen MacArthur only seven times, he discussed the general's egotism, selfishness, and rumors that he is afraid of flying. He went on to accuse MacArthur of ignorance of local conditions because of his lack of travel to Darwin, Australia, or Port Moresby, New Guinea, and a failure to consult with any of his component staff. Brett acknowledged at the beginning of the document, "I am partially biased in this case, due to certain personal relationships which have been apparently unavoidable." He doesn't specify which personal relationships, but he devoted a page of invective to Sutherland. Nonetheless, while reflecting personal enmity toward MacArthur's chief of staff, Brett provided golden advice for Kenney, "It is felt that a show-down early in the game with Sutherland might clarify the entire atmosphere."[7] Of course, Kenney took the opportunity to create such a confrontation as soon as he could, apparently to very satisfactory effect. The fact that Brett knew this was the right course, and even put it in writing, leaves the reader a bit stunned. Why didn't Brett face up to Sutherland himself? After all, he outranked Sutherland. Perhaps MacArthur's early affronts to Brett and Sutherland's continuous slights provoked Brett's umbrage so much that he was simply unable to overcome his resentment. If so, simplicity of spirit, as well as loyalty, failed him in this case.

General Brett was well versed in the doctrinal applications of airpower that today's Airmen call close air support, interdiction, reconnaissance, and air superiority. Indeed, Brett pushed hard for the meager forces at his disposal to accomplish all they could in the air superiority and reconnaissance arenas. MacArthur demanded interdiction, however, and Brett resisted because of his urge to husband his forces for more concentrated attacks in the future. This impulse makes sense and speaks well of Brett's tactical and operational expertise. The strategic value of using precious bombers that were being successfully employed for lucrative reconnaissance missions for small-scale strikes of predictably negligible effect was simply not worth the cost.

Brett's experience in the Pacific started under a cloud of Japanese air superiority. Lack of radar and early warning networks meant that his priceless fighter resources were frequently scrambled late or destroyed on the ground. This situation finally began to improve after the collapse of ABDACOM, when the Japanese found themselves overextended. When Royce led the strike on the Philippines, they took the enemy by surprise and encountered light and disorganized resistance. More strikes of this kind, carefully planned to create the best strategic effects, probably would have contributed to earlier exhaustion of the Japanese forces. Brett was likely correct, though, in his assessment that he did not have the resources for a sustained effort before the late summer of 1942. Thus, interdiction had to wait.

Air superiority, however, was bravely contested by the Allied air forces in Darwin and at Port Moresby. Although the forward deployed fighters and bombers suffered frequent air raids from the Japanese, they quickly learned to recover and prevent serious loss of life or equipment. They also became better at predicting the raids—negating the devastating element of surprise the Japanese had employed to such good effect at the beginning of the war. This good intelligence was fostered in part by Brett's use of the bombers that would otherwise have conducted interdiction to fly reconnaissance missions.

Brett's message traffic also showed his penchant for a less orthodox use of airpower—the transportation of personnel and equipment by air. Airlift, in modern parlance, was of great concern to Brett because of Australia's inadequate surface transportation network. Early on he discovered that the quickest and most reliable way to move items around the continent and forward to New Guinea was by air. Shipping provided a more robust capability for heavy loads, but it was slow and very vulnerable to Japanese air attack. There were not enough fighter assets available to protect shipping adequately, so important cargo had to be sent by air. Brett worked with Australia's civil aviation industry to secure as much airlift as he could from civilian as well as military sources, a practice which was continued by Kenney.

Considering the limited resources at his disposal and the doctrinal missions he was charged with performing, Brett showed a mastery of airpower as it related to the combat effort for the first months of the war in the Pacific theater. It appears he prioritized air missions properly and allocated combat aircraft and sorties in the most effective way possible, considering his arduous circumstances. Brett did not succeed as well in the way he organized the Allied air forces chain of command. His hesitation to leave Melbourne bespeaks a serious discomfort Brett felt about cooperation with the Royal Australian Air Force. In his briefing to Kenney, Brett carefully outlines his appreciation of the relationship between the US and Australian forces. The American tendency to "give little consideration" to the Australian land forces "has brought on quite a bit of trouble and is probably responsible for [Air Marshal William] Bostock's dissatisfaction with his certainly peculiar position . . ." as Allied air forces chief of staff.[8]

In selecting Bostock as his chief of staff, Brett had hoped to create a model he would duplicate throughout the theater, with an American Airman either in command or second in command, and an Australian airman filling the opposite role. Brett should have seen from his difficult relationship with Bostock, however, that such an arrangement would be hard at best, and doomed to failure at worst. The politics of the RAAF had already intruded into Brett's office under the aegis of the feud between Bostock and Australian air marshal Sir George Jones, who thwarted Bostock's ambitions by becoming the chief of the air staff. Of Bostock, Brett said, "He has no true concept of an Allied Air Force and is always suspicious that some action is going to be taken to deprive the Australians of what they have gained. There also appears to be a lot of interior politics of which we, as Americans, are not informed."[9] Bostock's attitude was similar to Tedder's; in addition to his personal disappointment at making way for Jones, he was understandably irritated to be subordinate to the recently arrived Brett.

This unsteady relationship was replicated throughout Brett's command, and Colonel Smith commented that when Brett imposed him on an Australian organization as chief of staff palpable resentment was the result. Kenney noticed when he arrived that the mixed combat crews had difficulty understanding each other, and the Australian weatherman's prediction of "rain" was misinterpreted to mean "rime," an icing condition that would have made flying very dangerous. Such misunderstandings were predictable, and they did nothing to foster a spirit of cooperation. One of Kenney's first moves was to reorganize the Allied air forces into separate American and Australian chains of command.[10]

Unity of command and economy of force, basic principles of war, are often very difficult to optimize in an alliance. Brett had already seen for himself that ABDACOM's lack of unity of effort, despite its nominal unity of command, had resulted in the uncoordinated loss of many lives and much irreplaceable equipment. Although the Australian and American interests were somewhat more conveniently aligned than those of the other ABDACOM Allies, Kenney's eventual solution of a combined headquarters for Allied strategic direction that commanded separate national entities at the operational level was much more successful in practice. While it sacrificed unity of command below the strategic level, unity of effort was maintained throughout the organization. This ultimately resulted in true economy of force, since each unit was performing its assigned mission in a more single-minded fashion.

Brett's combat execution, therefore, was stymied by a lack of organizational adaptation. In his care to avoid offending the RAAF, Brett suffered with an organization that was not suited to its combat mission. The key was to provide the Australians with high-level input to the air strategy, and this is what Kenney achieved with a combined strategic headquarters. MacArthur saw the lines of this organization almost immediately, when he described the Australians as prepared for coastal defense. Kenney also recognized this quickly, and tasked his Australian Allies with the mission they were best suited for. If Brett had organized his forces into national entities with combined strategic direction earlier, it is possible he would have been able to mount a more coordinated resistance to the Japanese advance. Such resistance might have made one or two months' difference in the grand scheme of the Allied push north toward the heart of Japan's empire.

Today's Airman is faced with many of the same challenges Brett found when he arrived in the Pacific. The resources provided will always be less than a conservative military man would array for the task at hand. Political conflict at the national level will tarnish or complicate relationships with allied or coalition partners. Even more serious, the enemy may find creative and unexpected ways to challenge friendly air superiority. While most Americans assume they will not face a credible threat in the air, there is no guarantee an air command will not have to contend with a determined surface-to-surface attack on friendly equipment and personnel. Indeed, most of our potential adversaries are quite willing to use unconventional means, perhaps up to and including weapons of mass destruction or weapons of mass effect, to achieve even a temporary superiority over friendly air forces. In fact, an air-to-surface threat is not implausible. With the advent of cheap guidance technology, an adversary could use our own global positioning system combined with an unpiloted or kamikaze-piloted aircraft to attack established air installations. The proliferation of high-quality, mobile surface-to-air missiles from the former Soviet Union also provides a source for well-financed adversaries to challenge friendly air dominance.

Such challenges will fall to the successors of men like General Brett. Their determination and preparation will be essential to success. Brett was undoubtedly both determined and prepared, but nonetheless his leadership faltered. Considering his obvious strengths, it appears he allowed his personality to interfere with his leadership task. Specifically, his struggle with self-discipline and pride led to a resentment which curtailed his ability to give General MacArthur the unflinching loyalty he demanded. On the exacting stage of combat execution, Brett performed admirably. His innate understanding of airpower and his unique talent as a supply expert allowed him to deliver semimiraculous performances with almost no resources. His ability to envision and direct airpower through the complex organizational web of Allied relationships was weak, however, and held him back from the success he might have achieved.

General Brett's dedication, patriotism, and moral rectitude are an excellent example to future generations of Airmen. His failings, such as they were, are equally pertinent as an illustration of how a very successful peacetime leader with many virtuous qualities can be faced with a confluence of circumstances so severe as to test even the will to succeed in combat. Ultimately, Brett must be counted as a success, both for his contribution to the growth and success of the Air Corps during its most strenuous test, World War II, and for his dedicated service to the United States in numerous positions of great responsibility.

While he was recognized for these contributions during his life and after his death, his story is unique because of the intriguing possibilities it arouses. Based on the research presented above, one might wonder what might have happened if things had been different. What if Brett had seen through his personality conflict with MacArthur and Sutherland and made a success of his leadership role in the Southwest Pacific area? How would his strong personality and bent toward logistics have impacted the course of the war? He was popular with the press, and had he achieved victory in the Pacific, it is conceivable he could have challenged other leaders of the newborn Air Force for critical responsibilities, perhaps also changing some of its fundamental directions. On the other hand, his unchanging bent of temper probably made conflict with MacArthur inevitable. Any glory that Brett might have gained from his efforts would have been jealously regarded by his commander in chief. Like General Brett, the judgment of history must also be a slave to the chain of command. In the words of General of the Air Force Henry H. Arnold, "General MacArthur arrived on 17 March 1942, and, from the first, it became evident that he and General Brett could not get along. Brett should have done the 'getting along,' as he was the junior."[11]

Notes

1. Brereton, *The Brereton Diaries*, 74.
2. *Merriam-Webster Online*.
3. Brett, "Oral History Interview," 73–74.
4. Green, "Prelude to Pearl Harbor Attack."
5. Ibid.
6. Ibid.
7. Brett, "Comments of Gen. Brett." Brett's description of Sutherland makes for an entertaining, if not entirely appropriate read. "He has assumed a knowledge in all matters which at times has made it most difficult for me.

93

He is arbitrary in his attitude and often renders decisions in the name of the C-in-C which it is felt the C-in-C has never had the opportunity to discuss. He is officious and rubs the majority of people . . . the wrong way, thereby creating a great deal of unnecessary friction. I consider him a bully who, should he lose his ability to say 'by order of General MacArthur' would be practically a nobody."

8. Ibid.

9. Ibid.

10. Kenney, *General Kenney Reports*, 53.

11. Arnold, *Global Mission*, 331.

Bibliography

Primary Sources, Archival Materials

Arnold, Henry H. "Brett Mission to England: Call number MIC-FILM 43835." Arnold Papers, Air Force Historical Research Agency (AFHRA), Maxwell AFB, AL, 1941.

———. "Correspondence (General): Alphabetical file, call number MICFILM 28050." Arnold Papers, AFHRA.

———. "Pre-War Correspondence: Call number MICFILM 28205." Arnold Papers, AFHRA, 1941.

Associated Press. "General Brett Is Awarded Flying Cross." Unlabeled newspaper, probably from Richmond, VA, 13 October 1942. Newspaper clipping, the Virginia Military Institute Archives (VMI), Lexington, Virginia.

Bostock, William. To chief of staff, Southwest Pacific Area. Letters, March–August 1942. MacArthur Memorial, Norfolk, VA.

Brett, Lt Gen Devol. "U.S. Air Force Oral History Interview: K239.0512-1273, Lieutenant General Devol Brett." Oral history, AFHRA, June 1981.

Brett, Lt Gen George H. Letters. Subject: Collected Correspondence from Commander, Allied Air Forces to General Headquarters, March–August 1942.

———. "Comments of Gen. Brett Re: Personnel, Etc." A compilation of statements given to Kenney on 3 August 1942. George C. Kenney Papers, Center for Air Force History, Bolling AFB, Washington, DC.

———. "Defense Procurements." *Aviation*, August 1940. Call number 168.3952-8, AFHRA, n.d.

———. Lincoln National Life Insurance Company. To chief of staff, United States Air Force. Letter, 8 February 1948. Collection of Brett-related papers in possession of Col Thomas E. Griffith, USAF.

———. To the Prime Minister of Australia. Letter, 17 March 1942. MacArthur Memorial, Norfolk, VA.

———. To Lt Col Withers A. Burress, VMI. Letter, 19 March 1938, the VMI Archives, Lexington, VA, n.d.

———. "U.S. Army Air Corps: The Combat Command Does the Fighting. The Air Corps Supplies the Guns, Planes, Men and Equipment to Do the Job." *Flying and Popular Aviation*, September 1941. Call number 168.7265-81, AFHRA, n.d.

———. "The MacArthur I Knew." *True Magazine*, October 1947. Call number 168.7103-14, n.d.

Churchill, Winston To Franklin D. Roosevelt. ABDACOM Command Arrangements. 1 February 1942. National Archives Textual Records, ARC identifier 195015.

Courtney, W. B. "Born to Fly." *Collier's*. 8 August 1942, 39. Article clipping, the VMI Archives, Lexington, VA.

Fitch, Brig Gen Burdette M. "Oral Reminiscences of Brigadier General Burdette M. Fitch." Oral history, August 1971, MacArthur Memorial, Norfolk, VA.

Fitch, Col Burdette M. To commander, Allied Air Forces. Letters, March–August 1942, MacArthur Memorial, Norfolk, VA.

"General Brett is America's Top Soldier in the Western Pacific." *Roanoke Times*. 7 February 1942, n.p. Newspaper clipping, the VMI Archives, Lexington, VA, n.d.

"George Howard Brett, Lt General, USA, AC, 1886–1963." Funeral Program, the VMI Archives, Lexington, VA, n.d.

Green, Murray. "Prelude to Pearl Harbor Attack (7 December 1941): World War II (Pacific Theater), Call number MICFILM 43811." AFHRA, 1988.

———. Collection, AFHRA, 1988.

Headquarters United States Army Air Services. *Personnel Report.* Melbourne, Australia: Office of the Commanding General, 13 May 1942. Collection of Brett-related papers in possession of Col Thomas E. Griffith, USAF. Document is now declassified.

Kenney, General George C. "Oral Reminiscences of General George C. Kenney." Oral history, MacArthur Memorial, Norfolk, VA, July 1971.

MacArthur, Gen Douglas A. Letters, March–August 1942. Subject: Collected Correspondence Regarding Lt Gen George H. Brett, MacArthur Memorial, Norfolk, VA.

Message. ABDA-162. ABDACOM. To Commanding General, Philippine Island, 1 February 1942. Collection of General

Brett's papers loaned to author by Maj Gen John Huston, USAF, retired.

———. ABDA-432. ABDACOM. To Adjutant General, War Department, Washington, DC. Collection of General Brett's papers loaned to author by Maj Gen John Huston, USAF, retired, 18 February 1942.

———. MacArthur. To Marshall, 30 June 1942. MacArthur Memorial, Norfolk, VA.

———. Marshall. To commander in chief, Southwest Pacific area, 14 May 1942. MacArthur Memorial, Norfolk, VA.

———. Marshall. To commander in chief, Southwest Pacific area, 29 June 1942. MacArthur Memorial, Norfolk, VA.

Military Record. "Military Record of Lt Gen George H. Brett." Personnel record, National Military Personnel Records Center, St. Louis, MO, n.d.

Record Group 18, National Archives and Records Agency. "Air Adjutant General Messages and Cable Division, General Arnold's Briefs of Messages 1942–1945, boxes 1–3." National Archives II, College Park, MD, n.d.

———. "Central Decimal Files 1917–1938, Air Corps Officers, file group 211, box 290." National Archives II, College Park, MD, n.d.

———. "Central Decimal Files 1917–1938, Air Corps Officers, file group 211, box 296." National Archives II, College Park, MD, n.d.

———. "Office of Information Services Periodicals, Air Force Service Journal 1945–1946, box 7." National Archives II, College Park, MD, n.d.

———. "Panama Air Depot France Field Canal Zone, 1933–1939, file group 000.4-300.4, box 2." National Archives II, College Park, MD, n.d.

———. "Panama Air Depot France Field Canal Zone, 1933–1939, file group 000.4-300.4, item 312." National Archives II, College Park, MD, n.d.

Roosevelt, Franklin D. To Winston Churchill. Draft announcement, 23 January 1942. National Archives Textual Records, ARC identifier 195022.

Smith, Frederic H., Jr. "U.S. Air Force Oral History Interview: K239.0512-903, Gen Frederic H. Smith, Jr." Oral history, n.d., AFHRA, June 1976.

"The Stratemeyer Papers: 168.7018-17." Collected papers, AFHRA, n.d.

Sutherland, Maj Gen Richard K. To commander, Allied Air Forces. Letters, March–August 1942. Subject: Collected Correspondence Regarding Lt Gen George H. Brett. MacArthur Memorial, Norfolk, VA.

VMI. "Cadet Information Card: George Howard Brett." Note card, the VMI Archives, Lexington, VA, n.d.

———. Collected Papers Regarding Lt Gen George H. Brett's death, VMI Archives, Lexington, VA, n.d.

Secondary Sources, Books, Journals, and Manuscripts

Arnold, H. H. *Global Mission.* New York: Harper & Brothers, 1949.

Brereton, Lewis H. *The Brereton Diaries: The War in the Air in the Pacific, Middle East and Europe, 3 October 1941–8 May 1945.* New York: William Morrow and Company, 1946.

Brownstein, Herbert S. *The Swoose: Odyssey of a B-17.* Washington, DC: Smithsonian Institution Press, 1993.

Copp, DeWitt S. *Frank M. Andrews: Marshall's Airman.* Washington, DC: Air Force History and Museums Program, 2003.

Craven, Wesley Frank, and James Lea Cate, eds. *The Army Air Forces in World War II.* Vol. 1, *Plans and Early Operations, January 1939 to August 1942.* Chicago: University of Chicago Press, 1948.

Cullum, Brevet-Major-General George W. *Biographical Register of the Officers and Graduates of the U.S. Military Academy at West Point, New York,* 1910 ed. Saginaw, MI: Seemann and Peters, 1910.

———. *Biographical Register of Officers and Graduates of the U.S. Military Academy at West Point,* 1920 ed.

———. *Biographical Register of Officers and Graduates of the U.S. Military Academy at West Point,* 1930–1940 ed.

Eastman, Linda A. *Portrait of a Librarian: William Howard Brett.* Chicago: American Library Association, 1940.

Eisenhower, David. *Eisenhower at War, 1943–1945.* New York: Random House, 1986.

Encyclopedia of Library and Information Science. Kent, Allen, and Harold Lancour, eds. New York: Marcel Dekker, 1970.

Futrell, Robert Frank. *Ideas, Concepts, Doctrine: Basic Thinking in the United States Air Force, Vol. 1 1907–1960.* Maxwell AFB, AL: Air University Press, 1989.

Generals of the Army and the Air Force. Washington, DC: Dunleavy, 1954. Vol. 2, no. 11 (December 1954): 2–3.

Howard, Michael. "Military Science in an Age of Peace." *Journal of the Royal United Services Institute for Defense Studies,* no. 119 (March 1974): 3–11.

James, D. Clayton. *The Years of MacArthur, Volume II, 1941–1945.* Boston: Houghton Mifflin Company, 1975.

Kenney, General George C. *General Kenney Reports: A Personal History of the Pacific War.* 1949. Reprint, Washington, DC: Office of Air Force History, 1987.

Long, Gavin. *The Six Years' War: A Concise History of Australia in the 1939–1945 War.* Canberra: Australian War Memorial and Australian Government Publishing Service, 1973.

MacArthur, General of the Army Douglas. *Reminiscences.* New York: McGraw Hill, 1964.

Manchester, William. *American Caesar: Douglas MacArthur 1880–1964.* Boston: Little, Brown and Co., 1978.

Miller, Roger G. "A 'Pretty Damn Able Commander' Lewis Hyde Brereton: Part II." *Air Power History* (Spring 2001).

National Cyclopedia of American Biography. Vol. F. New York: James T. White and Co., 1942.

Pogue, Forest C. "George C. Marshall: Global Commander." In *The Harmon Memorial Lectures in Military History.* Edited by Harry R. Borowski. Washington, DC: Office of Air Force History, 1988.

———. *George C. Marshall: Ordeal and Hope, 1939–1942.* New York: Viking Press, 1966.

Rogers, Paul P. *The Good Years: MacArthur and Sutherland.* New York: Praeger, 1990.

Rose, William Ganson. *Cleveland: The Making of a City.* Cleveland: World Publishing Co., 1950.

Shepard, LCDR Steven B. "American, British, Dutch, and Australian Coalition: Unsuccessful Band of Brothers." Master's thesis, Command and General Staff College, Fort Leavenworth, KS, 2003.

Tedder, Marshal of the Royal Air Force Sir Arthur William. *With Prejudice.* Boston: Little, Brown and Co., 1966.

Woollcombe, Robert. *The Campaigns of Wavell, 1939–1943.* London: Cassel, 1959.

Secondary Sources, Electronic

Fairchild Research Info Center & Maxwell/Gunter Comm Libraries Catalog AUL Index to Military Periodicals 1988–Current. https://sisko.au.af.mil.

Haller, Stephen A. "Aviation at Crissy Field." *National Park Service Web site.* n.p. 1 February 2004. http://www.nps.gov/prsf/history/crissy/crissyaf.htm.

Merriam-Webster Online. n.p. 3 May 2004. http://merriamwebster.com.

Miller, Dr. Roger G. Office of Air Force History. To Lt Col Douglas A. Cox. E-mail. Subject: General George Brett Thesis Questions, 16 April 2004.

USAF Museum Website, n.d., n.p., 21 May 2004, http://www.wpafb.af.mil/museum/research/bombers/b2-34.htm.

"U.S. Central Command History." *USSOUTHCOM* Web site. 28 February 2004, n.p. http://www.southcom.mil/pa/Facts/History.htm.

Wheat, John. "Contribution from John Wheat—Learning to Fly in the AEF." The Great War Society Website. 3 September 1917, n.p. 12 May 2004. http://www.worldwar1.com/tgwscontr/johnwheat1.htm.

Index